Quaker
Peace Stories

Northamptonshire Area
Quaker Meeting

First published: 2010

Published by Northamptonshire Area Quaker Meeting of the
Religious Society of Friends

Copyright © Northamptonshire Area Quaker Meeting

ISBN: 978-1-4461-3464-1

c/o Northampton Quaker Meeting House
Wellington Street, Northampton NN1 3AS

Printed by www.lulu.com

CONTENTS

CHAPTER 1

INTRODUCTION

This book of Quaker peace stories is the outcome of a much longer history. A religious commitment to peace has been at the heart of Quakerism since its origins during the seventeenth century English Civil War.

While some future Quakers fought in the war, others shared the conviction of George Fox and William Dewsbury that armed conflict was a denial of religious truth. In 2011 Quakers commemorate the 350th anniversary of the first collective declaration of the Quaker peace testimony, addressed to the restored monarch: "So we, whom the Lord hath called into the obedience of his Truth, have denied Wars and Fightings, and cannot again any more learn it. And this is a certain Testimony unto all the World, of the truth in our hearts." A few months earlier Margaret Fell expressed the positive side of Quaker peacemaking: "We are a People that follow after those things that make for Peace, Love and Unity, it is our desire that others' feet may walk in the same, and we do deny and bear our Testimony against all Strife and Wars."

Both the rejection of armed conflict and the promotion of active peace-making have strongly characterised the Religious Society of Friends since these early days. In 1693 William Penn urged his followers to remember that "A good end cannot sanctify evil means; not must we ever do evil, that good may come of it." In 1805, during the Napoleonic Wars, London Yearly Meeting advised Quakers to "Guard against placing your dependence on fleets and armies; be peaceable yourselves, in word and actions." In 1870 Quakers responded to the Franco-Prussian War by founding a medical and social relief service which ministered to both sides in the conflict. When the First World War broke out in 1914, the Quaker message was one of sorrow but also of determination to "search for a positive, vital, constructive message...a message of supreme love." And in 1938, as war once again loomed,

Yearly Meeting reaffirmed the historic peace testimony, reminding Quakers that "Peace is not a state of tranquillity, but a constant struggle."

The Quaker peace stories presented here are a reminder of the many different forms which the "struggle" for peace may take. They are also a reminder that not all Quakers have felt alike about peace and war. Opposition to war ranges across a wide spectrum of opinion, and Quakers, like everybody else, need to work out their own responses within different conflict situations. Not all Quakers have been conscientious objectors. Some have enlisted for military service, some have served in unarmed support of the armed services, others have refused all forms of war work and gone to prison as a result. In more recent years some Quakers have opposed war by challenging Cold War mythology and opposing nuclear weapons, while others have served the cause of peace by devoting their skills to work in developing countries.

In recent years Northamptonshire Quakers (with others) have taken an active local role in promoting fair trade and environmental causes, seeking inter-faith understanding, assisting asylum seekers, opposing the Iraq War and supporting a monthly peace vigil in Northampton town centre. In 2009 we developed a public exhibition, titled Quaker Roads to Peace, which reminded us of our strong peace-making heritage. This book has developed from the exhibition. We want to share the peace stories of local Quakers with the widest possible readership – not in any spirit of boastfulness, but rather in the cause of active peace-making for the future. We believe that it is vital to put stories of peace-making on the historical record, alongside the innumerable histories of war, and we hope that other Area Meetings may decide to compile similar books of oral and written testimony.

CHAPTER 2

LEONARD GRAY

Conscientious objector in World War II

Len Gray is a member of Northampton Local Meeting. He has written a personal account of his experience as a conscientious objector and has also recorded an extended interview. Both accounts are included here, together with a set of photographs taken during his wartime work with the International Voluntary Service for Peace. Together, these accounts provide insight into Len's personal decision-making and his early encounters with Quakerism.

Leonard Gray

PEACE STORY

From the age of fourteen I had begun to take a deeper interest in religion and particularly in the Anglo-Catholic church where I was a communicant and regular attender. I was a server and with the choir and other servers spent some summers on the estate of the Townshend family who allowed us to use some cottages and outbuildings at Raynham Hall near West Raynham. From there we travelled to Walsingham to visit the Anglican shrine of Our Lady of Walsingham. I seem to remember that I was not impressed by the shrine itself but the obvious devotion of the people tending the shrine and of the worshippers was impressive.

In 1938 the possibility of war began to seem very real and I was finding it more and more difficult to reconcile the teachings of Jesus with the concept of war. With the declaration of war in September 1939 I had to decide whether, holding this belief, I could accept service in the armed forces or whether I should be a conscientious objector.

Whilst I was agonising over this I discovered a colleague who had already determined that he would register as a conscientious objector (for political reasons) and in discussions with him I found out about various pacifist bodies. I began to read their literature. By sheer coincidence at this time I renewed my acquaintance with two old school friends who were attenders at the local Friends Meeting. I knew nothing about the Society of Friends at this time but soon learned of their peace testimony and that the warden of the local Meeting House had organised a weekly meeting for conscientious objectors and those who like me were finding it difficult to accept conscription. He offered only support, fellowship and information – never trying to steer anyone in any direction. Indeed it would have been useless to do so. If you did not really and sincerely believe in the cause of pacifism you would be unable to stand the social pressures which came with the label of "conscientious objector". He used to look over the statements we prepared for submission to the Tribunal. In mine I wrote that Jesus Christ was the revelation of God "to man". He suggested that perhaps I should say "in man". I was unable to do this simply because at that time I had not encountered the Quaker belief in "that of God in every man". Now of course I would write something very akin to this. My beliefs and faith have moved away from the orthodoxy I accepted at that time.

Eventually when my call-up papers came I registered as a conscientious objector. Although nobody in my immediate circle of family and friends was critical or condemnatory I received little help from my mother who, I think, could not understand what I was doing. I wonder now whether she ever discussed my action with anybody outside the family because I realise now that she would have been very embarrassed to admit that I was a "conchie". But my employer made it clear that whilst I would not be "forced" to go, he would like me to leave. I am still not sure why he felt like this, because he was on the whole a very fair-minded man, but there was no doubt about his desire to see the back of me.

The problem I had was what to do in a country gearing up for a war in which the whole of the population would be making sacrifices. It was almost impossible to find work which in some way or another was not helping the "war effort" and I wanted to find something constructive which would be an affirmation of my Christian values and a denial of the culture of destruction. In common with other COs [conscientious objectors] I looked for ways of making a constructive contribution to the community. I had heard of the International Voluntary Service for Peace and their work camps and I also discovered that they were starting a re-afforestation scheme in Kershope Forest in north Cumberland. Kershope is a small adjunct to Kielder Forest. I applied for a place and was accepted. Early in 1940 for the first time in my life I left the places and sights and sounds which had been my environment for nineteen years and headed for a life and work which were completely unknown to me. My two school friends came to Euston station to see me off on the overnight train to Carlisle. I never saw them again but I heard later that one of them, Tom Hayley, joined the FAU [Friends Ambulance Unit] and went with the Unit to China. I was never able to find out what happened to my other friend.

My decision to go to Kershope was a result of my desire to do something constructive. There were other opportunities to do this (e.g. Friends Ambulance Unit) but they required participants to finance themselves and this I could not afford. At Kershope I would be paid the same weekly wage as a private soldier. In some way this made me feel that I was not taking advantage of not being in the services. In fact it was not until some months later that a tribunal in Carlisle "decided" that my objection was "conscientious" and agreed that I should not be conscripted.

Most of the other volunteers were middle class and had attended university and through them I became aware of a world of literature and intellectual achievement previously unknown to me and this period was one of learning and reading voraciously authors I had never before heard of – John Murray is one that springs to mind. I was also conscious of a great sense of well-being due no doubt to the hard physical work entailed in working in the forest. There was no machinery and we dug drains, planted trees, weeded young plantations and nursery beds all by hand. There was much humour and comradeship in the work and in our small community.

I remember the experience as a boy from the East End of London learning about the cultivation of trees, helping farmers at harvest time, and digging potato clamps. I began to feel more confident and this I think must have become apparent because I was deputed to go to the local farmers and arrange for a supply of potatoes to see us through the winter – hence the building of clamps. My recollections of these occasions was that all negotiations had to be preceded by at least half an hour of discussion about the weather and other topics before we got down to the business of arranging a contract between us. We lived in a small hamlet called Grahams Onsett and it was part of my duties each week to cycle into the nearest town – Longtown – to cash a cheque at the bank to pay the volunteers' allowance and draw cash for the housekeeping.

(I have visited Grahams Onsett since – in 2001 – when Jerry, hearing of my wish to revisit this scene, took me on a pilgrimage to Kielder Forest and through Grahams Onsett to Kershopefoot and Newcastleton and then back to Carlisle and so home.)

The earnings of the Group were paid into a common fund from which living expenses were deducted together with the sum of seven shillings per week for each volunteer. This was the pay of a private soldier and meant that we did not benefit economically from our privileged status. The balance of our earnings was sent to IVSP Leeds head office to be used for similar schemes.

Eventually the Forestry Commission decided to dispense with our services and the Kershope scheme was closed. We were all transferred to another scheme in Plaistow, East London., where we formed a demolition squad to take down buildings which had become dangerous having suffered bomb damage. The work was also done without the aid of machinery except for the lorries which carried away the rubble. This manual labour aspect of the work reflected the IVSP slogan "Pick and Shovel Peacemaking".

I stayed with this squad for about a year. During this time I began to learn more about Friends and visited Friends House from time to time to take part in meetings and a conference with other peace workers. I began to attend Meeting for Worship.

I then learned of the work of the Friends War Victims Relief Committee. I cannot now remember precisely how but I began to work for them in their storage depot in Canonbury. Here we collected and distributed the furnishings, furniture and equipment for the children's evacuation hostels which they had opened throughout the country. Delivering this equipment by motor vehicle took me to parts of the country that I had not previously visited. The overnight stops after delivery meant that we spent many long hours in discussion and I became aware of the breadth of vision which Quaker workers shared but which was new to me. I also had the privilege of spending a weekend at Charney Manor with other Relief workers. I still felt myself to be an Anglo-Catholic and attended Mass whenever I could but I began to find that Quakers somehow had a better grasp on the reality of religion.

In 1944 I decided to return to "civilian" life and I left the Friends Relief Service as it was then known. I returned to the City and a job with a small shipping company and later with the Netherlands Shipping and Trading Committee – the commercial arm of the Netherlands Government in exile.

During this time I met Betty through the introduction of a mutual acquaintance, and with her occasionally attended Baptist services. The worshippers were enthusiastic but it did not appeal to me. Betty also was beginning to feel disillusioned with the Baptists. The War ended in September 1945 and in December 1945 we were married and decided we needed to find a church which could accommodate both of us.

RECORDED PEACE STORY (December 2009)

In the beginning...

Can you tell me about the origins of your pacifism?

Well the short answer to that is – there was never any suggestion of that at school, but I was a member of a church and I believed in the teachings of that church. It seemed to me, as I began to think for myself at about sixteen, the teachings of the church were at odds with what they actually did – certainly in terms of war. At that time, don't forget that war – the possibility of another war – from 1937-38 onwards was becoming quite real. So it wasn't so much a question of doing it hypothetically. You were thinking that maybe the time would come – we don't know when, but in a few years time – that that would happen. But at that time I wasn't thinking about what I would do, just recognising the fact that the world situation was such that a war could happen. In a very naive sort of way, I must say! I was, by that time, say seventeen or something like that.

What kind of school did you go to?

An ordinary elementary school, then I went to a grammar school. Funnily enough, the school – before I got there – had just disbanded its cadet force.

Which church did you join?

Anglo-Catholic. I did all the altar serving and that sort of thing. I was quite keen and there were quite a lot of boys of my age there doing the same thing.

Did you have any discussion groups at the church?

There was a Youth Club run by a lay worker who arranged social meetings in the Parish Room on Sunday afternoons. All the altar servers and some of the choir attended and we usually just sat and talked. Tea was served and after the meal the lay worker would deliver a little homily on what I would now call Christian Faith and Practice: although his views would not now, I think, find space in the Quaker Book. There might be some questions after his talk but certainly we would never have discussed pacifism.

Did you read about pacifism?

Yes. Much publicity was given to Oxford University undergraduates' resolution to refuse "to take up arms for King and Country". At this time, also, Dick Sheppard I think published a letter in the (then) *Manchester Guardian*, requesting all those who wanted to support pacifism to write to him renouncing their support of war. There was a huge response and a meeting was held in the Albert Hall from which the Peace Pledge Union was formed. I remember these events but I cannot remember whether or not I became a member. There was also Donald Soper and the MP for East Ham George Lansbury who spoke out for pacifism. I do not remember how much my reading about these events affected my own beliefs, but they would have been in my thoughts as I struggled with the development of my own attitude. Something must have happened, but I can't pin it down, which concentrated my thoughts about it.

Probably a combination of things?

The fact was that I was quite firm and determined in my beliefs, not just in going to church. There was one man who caused a stir, a preacher... I can't remember his name. I think that focused my attention on it. There were very few people around who would have taken the same stance at that time. Later on I began to meet other people. Funnily enough, I was saying to Betty, it's incredible that, in quite a small area of Bethnal Green, there were three people who were conscientious objectors, who were pacifists. And we didn't know each other, until afterwards. When I felt that this was what I wanted to do, it was quite by accident – even now I can't remember what happened – I met a guy I'd been at school with. He wasn't a Quaker but he was involved with what was then the Bedford Institute (they've all gone now) which was in Barnet Grove. There was a Friends Hall in Barnet Grove, Bethnal Green (it's gone now). I don't know how – I suppose in discussing these things, what he felt came out. He wasn't necessarily saying at that time that he would be a conscientious objector. We didn't think in those terms, you know. He and I and one other man – sometimes it was three of us, sometimes it was four. I would go to church on Sunday morning, and they would go to Meeting or whatever and we'd meet up afterwards and take a walk, a Sunday morning walk, usually around Victoria Park, and that was when we had these deep-seated discussions, and solved the problems of the world you know, at that age! It was then that I began to develop more.

When it came to the crunch and I actually made the decision, there was nobody around at all. What had happened to them I don't know. I think one guy had joined the Army. They went off somewhere. In any case, when I decided to go to Kershope [as a volunteer forestry worker] two of them – one of them was Tom Hayley who joined the Friends Ambulance Unit – they came to Euston with me to see me off on the train which took me off to Kershope. I never saw them again. By the time I got back to London they had gone. All I know is that Tom Hayley went to China, that's all. I never met him again.

The outbreak of war and meeting other pacifists

Where were you when war broke out?

I was at home, working. It wasn't any particularly brilliant job, I was just working as a clerk in London.

How did you feel on the day when you had to go and make your statement as a CO?

That was a bit nerve-racking. But like a lot of things in life, you have to face them, and so you do. It was – I don't know how to put it – it was a test in a way.

But you'd made your mind up in advance?

Oh yes, there was no doubt about it. I must have had, in the back of my mind, I must have read and got other information as well because I did that too confidently. I knew what to do when I got there, that's the point. So somehow I must have been in touch with other people who also knew, because I remembered the phrase, "I wish to register as a conscientious objector." It was not mine, it was something that I had found out that you had to say.

There were associations of COs?

Yes, that's right. Most Christian faith groups had "peace" committees and most of these worked with the Central Board for Conscientious Objectors. The Fellowship of Reconciliation also was helpful. There were bodies, Quakers among them, that were set up to help and advise. And of course Charles Howarth was the Warden at the Bedford Institute and he was a Quaker. If I had to mention anybody who affected my life, I would say he did. He was a good man, a very good man. He went down, at some stage, to the Bernard Baron homes in Sussex, for elderly people. I think he became a Warden down there. Once upon a time I was thinking of going down there to try and track him down, but I never did. I heard about him from these two friends I had met, because they were – I don't know how serious they were in terms of their religious ideas, but they had a very good social club going, and Charles Howarth, whilst running the social club, also made it clear what the basis for his reason for doing it was. So they understood that it wasn't just do-goodery, as it were. He set up a kind of social evening where anybody who had thoughts of becoming a conscientious objector, or was having difficulty in reconciling the idea of war, could go along and chat. He never tried to proselytise, we just chatted about our various experiences and about things in general. What is amazing – I can remember this room – it was about four times as big as this, and there were men all round the room. I mean, in that small space, all of them interested. How many of them actually became pacifists I don't know.

I met one of them later on. When I was working for the Friends, for a time I stood in for one of the workers who was ill, down at one of the evacuation hostels, down in Somerset, near the Foxes' place, Gerbestone Manor. Now that's been taken over and it's a conference suite. The Foxes were the main people and Quakers there: they were running a hostel for evacuated children on their land. We cared for the children, washing and bathing them and their clothes, and in a caravan on the site we cooked meals for them. That was one of the things that I did, but only for a short time because I was only standing in while I was waiting for something else.

What I was saying was that while I was there – this is interesting – you've probably never heard of Spiceland, have you? Spiceland Training Centre, it was set up by south-western Friends. During the War a lot of people went there to train for relief work, and one of the friends I'd had in Bethnal Green was there. So I cycled over one day. It wasn't too far away and so I cycled over and met him, and I think I stayed the night and came back the next day. I met Stanley Smith who was the farm manager there and then met him again and his wife Marjorie again in Ilford when Betty and I settled there after the War. He was the clerk of Ilford Meeting. He was a great help in introducing us to Friends in the Monthly Meeting and we remained friends until he died two years ago.

Just to tell you – what amazes me, in that area, where you would not expect such a high proportion of people who thought that way, they were dotted all over the place. They weren't conscientious objectors, but pacifists. But when you started thinking about it yourself for the first time, you were very low. But gradually, of course, as the War went on all this began to disappear. What I'm talking about now... something happened while the War was on. As the effects of the War took effect people began to disappear: called up, or evacuated, or moved off to be somewhere safer. So in the end, I probably had... except for those two people who saw me off, and one of those wasn't a pacifist, I mean there was nobody around at all.

Telling the boss

You said your employer wasn't very sympathetic?

Well he was an ex-Army officer. I happened to know that one of his nephews, I think it was, had volunteered for the Army. Also I know that he brought his gun and Sam Browne belt, a leather strap which supports the holster, and he brought his old one up to give to his nephew. Well he had this in his hand while I was telling him that I was going to register as a conscientious objector! I had to tell him because he would expect or know that I would be called up, and he would wonder what was happening if I didn't tell him. I think he was surprised as well, because in the time between the start of the war and my going I had taken part in the neighbourhood fire watch and ARP [Air Raid Precautions]. You went about and extinguished small fires started by incendiary bombs and that sort of thing. We didn't have very much to do where we were, but I was doing it and he knew that. So he was quite surprised. To my mind it was something quite different to do that.

What did he say when you told him?

I think he wasn't critical of me, funnily enough, but he was critical of the movement. Because I said to him, "Well I don't want to shirk everything. I'm going up to Cumberland and I shall join an organisation that will pay me a Private's pay and I will be working quite hard work in a forest there." He said, "Where did you say it was?" I said, "Cumberland." "They couldn't have found a safer place, could they?" I said, "I don't know about that." "Oh", he said, "I'm not saying anything about you." I think he respected my decision. They all knew in that office that I was quite principled as regards my religious things. I remember once, we had two or three in an office and I was the younger and I had to answer the telephone one day and the boy said, could he speak to Mr whatever-it-was. So, "It's message for you." This guy said, "Tell him I'm not here." I said, "I can't do that!" They couldn't believe it:

"Why not?". I said, "Well that's lying." So they knew the sort of person I was, so I suppose it wasn't all that much of a surprise.

Forestry work and bombsite clearance

How did conscientious objectors know where to go? How did you find out about the forestry work?

Well I don't know how I found out about IVSP (International Voluntary Service for Peace) but I must have seen something or heard something. I remember going to see somebody, I think it was up in Islington somewhere, to talk about what they were doing and whether they would be interested in my joining to do something. But, it's a terrible thing to say, but I can't remember anything about that except that it actually took place. As a result of that meeting I volunteered to join that particular group in Cumbria.

It must have been very hard physical work in the forest?

Honestly you wouldn't recognise what I looked like there, after a few months of working there. The point was that IVSP – their motto was "pick and shovel peace-making". Because all the work they did was manual, quite hard manual work. And Pierre Ceresole, who founded the movement Service Civil International, he spoke about it almost as though there was some kind of sacramental nature in working together. His idea was that people working together, doing that kind of work, would form bonds and it would help towards peace. But of course once the war broke out the camps were entirely English, or British. I think that's how I found out about it, somebody must have told me about IVSP or I must have read about it somewhere. I think I had an enquiring mind!

So you did adapt to the hard work?

Well, the first summer it was very hot, a heat wave. We couldn't strip off because we'd have burnt too much, but I was working with my sleeves rolled up and it got to the point where they got so burnt that I couldn't put my sleeves down again. It was quite hard. But apart from that, somewhere I've seen a description of the work we were doing. I wish I could reproduce it but I can't. It was quite hard.

Who was in charge of you?

The leader of the scheme was that chap Ramsey Bramham, who's in that photograph, the chap smoking a pipe. He was the leader in the Centre. We had a business meeting, I think once a week, to discuss anything... that sort of thing. It was a community, to that extent. But the work was organised by the forester who was employed by the Forestry Commission. Either he spoke to us himself, or through a ganger. So we had with us, while we were working, a ganger who would tell us what to do. And the poor chap also had the job of showing us how to do it!

Did he make sure you were all working hard?

Well no, that was never a problem. I'm not kidding, that was never a problem. In fact, I'll tell you another story about that. We were learning to dig drains, see, we were doing this by hand. Nowadays what we did would be frowned on, afforestation and the way we did it, but it was the thing at the time. They took a site which had a slope on it for a drain, and you dug a trench from top to bottom, following the lie of the land. And then you put what they called herringbone drainage. Then you brought the trenches in like this, and these trenches were at ten-foot intervals. When you stood in one, your feet were on the bottom and the sides would be – [at least a yard]. So you were going quite deep and the way you did that was with what you called a Tommy spade, which is a spade with a point like that and a cross bar, and the top of the blade is turned over so that you can put your foot on it. Then there was a line. I mean, let's suppose you want to dig a drain just here – there'd be a line, the ganger would put a line down there and you'd have to measure out... I think he said, "It's got to be two feet away from you." You'd start off with this thing of pushing in, as far down as you could go. Pull it back, then go on again like that. I mean in the end, to do it properly you were almost dancing along! It was very hard.

But you didn't need chivvying to work hard?

No, it was conscience. We weren't doing it for pay. When you'd done the two sides, you had to go through crossways now, and cut between the two lines so that you produced a sod, tip that up, and when you'd done the whole drain you then went along with another thing which was like a kind of pitch fork that angles that way down, like that, bang it into the hod, pick it out and sling it up. That would be five feet from the drain, and the next one had to be on the edge of the drain. And then, the final thing was you had to get into the drain with a spade about that wide and level it off. We were close enough to each other working, generally, to be able to talk but I don't remember what we actually said.

Were your companions like yourself, like-minded people from a similar background?

Well one or two were boys from the kind of background that I had, but most of them were more middle class and more... Certainly some of them were at the university, in fact I think one of them was a university Reader. So you had quite a spread of intellectual...

Were most of them Christians?

That's something I can't remember. All I know is that most of them used to attend a Meeting for Worship on Sunday mornings.

Were they Quakers?

Well no... I suppose it's inevitable when you have a mixed company that a Meeting after the manner of Friends is the simplest way of getting everybody together.

So some were Quakers, presumably?

I suppose so, I don't know.

You did quite a lot of other jobs too?

Oh well, that was in the early part, that was when I first started. I went up there for a year or so, more than that, long enough to go through the whole cycle of the thing. There was part of the time when we couldn't work, because the fells were under snow. Changing the subject, Jerry and I drove up there three or four years ago now, and I was walking alongside the places where we'd been.

Were the trees still there?

Oh yes, and also there was an interesting thing – there was a place called Cuddy's Hall – a lot of places with the name Cuddy up there, because of St Cuthbert's body, he was reported to have rested there while he was on the way to Carlisle Cathedral. Cuddy's Hall, when I was there, was a broken-down old cottage in which we used to shelter occasionally if it rained. But I mean it wasn't something we could do permanently! But when we went up there a few years ago, someone had bought it and rebuilt it, and it was a magnificent country home.

Then, for a time all went well and in fact... just to pick up the point you made about being willing to work, and that sort of thing, at one point up there some of the locals went on strike and they wouldn't work in the weather, the weather was so bad. The forester was insisting they should work, and they were saying, "No, the weather's too bad." And Ramsey Bramham went and spoke to him. We were in a difficult position because if he told us to work we didn't want to say no. On the other hand we didn't want to weaken the position of the workers. So in the end – I don't quite know how the discussion went on, but Ramsey Bramham went to talk to him about it and I think he was pointing out that it would be very difficult for us to say no, if they didn't want to work. And he also discussed with him the actual state of weather, and in the end the forester agreed that on that day we wouldn't be working – all of us! Anyway, it does show that we were keen on working.

Then we left there – the Forestry Commission decided they'd had enough, didn't want to do any more planting. Because while we were there we planted, and all that business. We also worked in Kielder for a time, and broke some sort of record planting trees, thousands of trees in that time. Anyway,

IVSP... I don't know how they arranged this, but we came back, we all came to London – that [photos] was pictures of us moving – and set up in Plaistow, and went round bomb shelters trying to build in facilities that would make life in the shelters easier. One of the things was lavatories. There were lavatories with no doors on them, that sort of thing, and we would go round fitting doors and other amenities as well. As I said, sometimes I went out with the nightshift to take the tea or sandwiches round to the people in the shelters.

Quite a change of scene?

Oh yes, but it was still hard. And also – I suppose you've seen the result of a bomb falling, in terms of physical damage? In that part of the world there were a large number of buildings which had been damaged but were not completely destroyed. But they were dangerous, and so the other job which we got there was demolishing these dangerous structures. So then we became navvies! I was saying to Betty, before I went there... I still have a slight fear of heights, I couldn't believe I could do it. At one point I was wheeling a wheelbarrow full of bricks and rubble across a gap at least as wide as this room, if not wider, on a plank about that wide! You'd get to the edge, and down below there was a lorry backed up to receive it, and you tipped it up, then went back again. And you know...well!!

Meeting the Quakers

How did you come in contact with Quakers?

I don't know how that happened. I think at some stage or another, in the course of working with IVSP, I must have met Quakers. I must have heard about them because the Friends did have, now and again have a conference, a meeting. I remember being up in Friends House once, I remember one in particular, being in this room with other conscientious objectors. And I suppose I must have talked to people and discussed things, what they were doing and that sort of thing, and heard about the job they were doing, and suggested... and made an application to join. To this day I cannot remember meeting anybody from the Society of Friends who asked me any questions about what I was doing, or whether I wanted to join. And yet, I finished up living with a group of Friends in Canonbury where we used to have a store with furniture, and we used to take it in, go round and collect it. People used to give us a lot of stuff, take it into the store and then in due course you'd get a note from Friends House of a hostel that was being set up, or had been set up even, but generally speaking in the process of being set up, and they wanted some items of furniture. And we'd load it onto this horse box and drive wherever we had to go. Get there, unload it, set it all up, then come back and start again. That was a very fruitful time as far as I was concerned, in terms of broadening my outlook on life. At that stage most of the people were, I think, university students and they had a library which I had access to. I found myself reading all sorts of things, didn't understand most of it, but as I grew older, later on in life, I was able to gradually, you know...

Was there a religious dimension to working with Friends?

As far as I was concerned I was only just considering what I already felt I had done. It was difficult at that point to go to church. I think it was a question of finding a church. It could have been the hours, yes. But nevertheless, I mean, what was happening was that in the house at Canonbury where we were living, we had a regular speaker, and I think that was what was beginning to... usually a speaker of that sort, though not necessarily a Quaker. Donald Soper came and spoke, and he wasn't a Quaker. Gradually I began to feel, you know, the arguments began to filter into my mind... you can never pinpoint these things.

Nobody tried to convert you?

No, no. I guess we probably talked about it quite a lot. Yes, I'm sure we did.

Then you ended up working for the Netherlands government?

Yes. It came to a point where I think what was available at that point with Friends was disappearing. Why, I don't know precisely. And also I think it came to the point that I had to face up to the fact that I needed to earn some money. Because I'd been living on seven shillings a week, my mother was living alone, the other children were at home and also my brother had gone into the Navy and my sister was in the Land Army, the other one was married. And so it was getting a bit sort of dicey. So I thought I ought to try and get back into work. And I discovered – this was the Netherlands government in exile, you know – and this organisation was running the Merchant Navy fleet for the government, while they were in this country. And so I thought, "Well, it's a bit of a compromise but nevertheless we need the merchant fleet to get food here and that sort of thing." So I went along and spoke to someone, and eventually got an appointment and told them what I'd been doing and they were quite happy to take me on.

They weren't prejudiced against COs?

Well I don't know whether they were or not, but I think they just wanted staff, to be honest.

A point of principle

There's something I want to tell you that I couldn't tell anybody. Only Betty knows, nobody else knows. I know that if I had been conscripted I wouldn't have been called up because my eyes are too bad. I'm almost blind in one eye and I knew from talking to people who'd been in that situation in areas where they came across people who'd been physically examined, that sort of thing, that there was no chance I would be called up. I knew that, but I thought, "Well I can't sort of..." [laughs]. Well, what would it have meant if I'd said, "Well OK..."? If I'd been conscripted and they decided I was of no use in war service, I would then be directed to a job. And I couldn't see much difference between that and going to fight in the Army. But if I could choose it myself, this is the funny thing about it, that's different. The odd thing about these things is that during my time in London, when I was living in London with other Friends, doing this sort of work, at some time or other I had to spend some time with Friends, working in Friends House, not for long, but for a time. And the staff of Friends House were fire-watching. And it became compulsory to do fire-watching, not by the Friends but by the government. And immediately the fire watchers said, "Well, we're not going to do it." They said, "Oh! Why not?" And they said, "It is quite different to be compelled to do this job, than to volunteer to do it." In the end I think we had another talk and think about it and said, "Well, maybe this is something where we can make an exception." But it was that kind of atmosphere.

Tribunals

If I may go back to the Tribunal, when you registered as a conscientious objector, you eventually were called up to a Tribunal. And you submitted a statement. Charles Howarth saw my statement, and had a look at it. He didn't alter it or anything. Anyway, when eventually you were called to your Tribunal you had to go up and it was like being in a court of law. And they asked you all sorts of things about what you'd been doing and what your beliefs were, that sort of thing. And it so happened that the parish priest also sent a letter saying what sort of person I'd been beforehand, so they'd have some idea that I wasn't just wangling it. But there were three things they could do to you. They could say you were absolutely excused, conditionally exempted, or you failed and in that case you would be conscripted, or you went to prison. I met several people afterwards who had been in prison because they wouldn't accept the fact. The other thing was that there was a strand of belief which considered the war was unjust on political grounds, rather than religion. And political conscientious objectors didn't have much chance of getting exemption. No, they had no chance at all – or very few. Very many didn't, and they had to go to prison. But what I'm trying to say is that if you belonged to one of the "peace churches" and you appeared before a Tribunal, you had hardly any questions at all. No matter what you'd done in the past, whether you'd supported pacifism or not. Some Quakers weren't pacifists. There were other peace churches as well, but they didn't get quite the same treatment. There were some

– was it Moravians? – who refused on the grounds of their religious belief in the same way, but they got a much harder time. I think it was just a hangover from what the Quakers had done in the previous war, with the Friends Ambulance Unit. Anyway, that's what happened and in my case they accepted me if I continued to do forestry work. So I thought to myself, "I could appeal, but what's the point? I've got what I want and they're only saying this because they don't want to say it is political, they don't want to say you're completely exempt. You're here doing forestry work, so you might as well carry on."

Did they come after you when you finished the forestry work?

I told them what I was doing. I said, "I'm going down to Plaistow to work with..." (what we were doing), and left it at that. I never heard so I just assumed that was alright.

Attitudes to COs

Did you encounter hostility from anybody because you were a CO?

No, I suppose the fact that I was known... I mean my family – I don't know, I mean they never ever said, apart from my employer. It was a big thing, people in the office all knew what I was doing, and it was OK. Funnily enough – it's incredible, this – in the office there was another man who was a conscientious objector. That'll be my influence, everywhere I go..! Yes, he in fact eventually joined a non-combatant unit. He and I, until I left there, were quite sort of chummy. I was trying to think... you see the thing was, once I realised what the situation was I naturally gravitated towards people who were thinking like I did. I didn't find them at first, but gradually I began to find out there were people around who were thinking like I did. At first I didn't know anybody. There was some break in my attendance at church, I can't think whether I was ill or what. The family moved and I went with them, and it took a while to get back into the rhythm of going to church. By the time I got back the whole thing had changed. It was only a matter of a few months. In that time boys had just disappeared, all the boys of my age had just gone.

Becoming a Quaker

So after the War, you joined the Society of Friends?

Well, what happened there was, in 1945, when I'd met Betty for some time, we got married. Of course she knew I was an Anglican and I knew she was a Baptist, and we talked about it and said, "We've got to find somewhere we can both go to." And so I said, "Well, I wouldn't mind going to the Friends Meeting." And although she hadn't been a regular Attender, she knew of Friends because, I think, something called a Friends Youth Club had been very active in the area where she had been living. So one Sunday morning we arrived at the local Friends Meeting House, to find a Meeting in progress! So we went home again. The next Meeting we realised it started earlier, and the next Sunday morning we went and got there in time, and from that moment onwards we went to Friends Meetings. But this is another story.

We formed some friendships there, for example, that lasted for life. The last person I can think of that we met there, was a friend of ours with his family for years and years. We kept in touch, all through sixty-odd years, and every now and again we met, either at Friends House or we wrote or telephoned. His wife died a long time ago, but he died about two years ago now. The awful thing was that I'd lost touch with him for the first time. So I tracked him down eventually, you know, took the last place he'd been at and gradually found out where he was. He was in Peterborough and Peterborough Friends gave me his address. So I rang him up and I finally discovered he was very, very ill. He didn't say in so many words, but he was. So I said to Jerry, "Some time, give me a lift up to Peterborough, I want to go and see this Friend." Before we could do it, he died. This guy was a Member, so with him we started going as Attenders to Monthly Meetings and that sort of thing, and gradually getting into the Society. In the end I said to this guy, "I really would like to apply for membership now. I think I've reached the stage now where I know where my religious priorities lie. I can't go on thinking of myself as a member of the Church of England anymore." So I made an application and in due course I was visited. In those days it was different to what it is now. And they accepted me. So that was somewhere between 1945 and 50, I suppose.

Was the peace testimony an important part of your decision?

It must have been a strong element, but I wouldn't have said it was the only or the main thing. Yes, it must have been part of it, I'm sure.

Quaker work since the War

How has the peace testimony been part of your life since the War?

To be honest with you, I didn't do much about peace. But once I was a member of the Society of Friends and became active, I did a lot of work in terms of housing. One of the things which I did was to interest myself in housing, and in Banbury one of the things we did was to form the Banbury District Housing Coalition, which was a coalition of all the churches. But the meeting which suggested this should be done was set up by Banbury Meeting. Betty was a Clerk. And so each church appointed a representative to attend another meeting to try and see how far we should go. And I remember that I went along.

We had one or two meetings and I could see we were getting nowhere, it was all just words, so I went back home one night and decided that we had to set down what we were doing and how we were going to do it. And I wrote out, typed out the constitution and aims of this body and then it started. And then what happened was this. We were doing a lot of thinking and discussing and talking about what we could do, and at one of the meetings was a man who'd had experience of this kind of thing somewhere else. I said to him, "I thought we were going to... I don't mind doing the work", I said, "but I thought we were going to try and whip up money and give it to other people to do the work." He said, "What can we do?" I said, "What sort of things would you do now?" "Well", he said, "The thing I would do would be to set up a rent guarantee scheme." And so I found out about rent guarantee schemes.

We had a meeting one Sunday morning and I said, "Well, I've promised on your behalf to support a rent guarantee scheme." It was amazing, everyone rallied round, and so we set up this organisation and its first job was guaranteeing the rents to landlords who wouldn't take on people whom they thought were either suspect or couldn't afford the rent. I discovered afterwards that ours was the only voluntary scheme in the country. What I found so delightful was that when we decided to do it we said, "Well, we need some money, if we're going to guarantee rent it needs money." And so we wrote a letter to every church and every priest, saying what we were doing and asking if they could help with a collection or give some money. And I thought we needed – I don't know how much we needed to sort the first batch of rent, whatever it was, it was in the neighbourhood of £3000. And I stood up in the Meeting one morning and told them we'd set this up and I'd promised that they would support it. And we raised this £3000 and I was delighted that the Friends Meeting provided almost the whole of that. The reply from the other churches was very poor. The Salvation Army were doing something like that anyway. So it was Friends, members of the Meeting mostly, who got ready the scheme. So, not peace, but that sort of thing.

Remembering the War

How do you feel about Remembrance Day now? Do you take part in commemorations?

Well I don't really, I'm very ambivalent about it. It's difficult to take part in the official services because they are so militaristic. Now and again you get the enlightened person, or parson, who talks about *all* the people who were killed in the War, including others, not just... But so often the parade is of all those people who fought, or were in the Army. And quite rightly, I mean they were there, they did what they thought was right. It's for them. But it's not something I can join in, because after all I don't believe in what they did. I mean I accept the fact they did it, and I accept the fact that it cost them perhaps more than it cost me to be a conscientious objector. But you know it's not part... It's difficult to explain, but if I remember, I remember all the things that happened, you know, the civilians and everything that happened. I don't like the way... you were talking about soldiers coming home, I don't like the way it's sort of ambushed to become a militarist operation. That's what it is. I mean the laying of a wreath at the Cenotaph, obviously it's done by the King or the Queen.

It doesn't sound as if your convictions have really changed, since all those years ago?

Oh no. Once or twice I've thought to myself, "Maybe there's a justification for doing that", on a particular occasion. But then I always come back, "No, there isn't." In the long run, in a situation like that, of conflict, whatever decision you make, whether to take part or not, is going to be painful. And if you decide, if a group of people decide, that rather than take life, they will submit to some kind of invasion or something like that, that's painful, that's very painful. It could mean loss of life for them. But if they resist, and there's a war, that's also painful, and there's loss of life. And it's a difficult decision to make. But I don't... I've never really decided, I've never really thought to myself, that it's right. In the long run it all comes down to one thing, and that is that if I were to say "Yes, this armed conflict is right", then I'd have to be prepared to kill somebody. And I'm not.

Photographs: Kershope, 1940-41

Conscientious objectors: Leonard Gray (front left), Ramsey Bramham
(centre, with pipe).

Grahams Onsett, where IVSP forestry workers lived. Women
volunteers helped with cooking.

Leaving Kershope for Plaistow. The journey took two days in a horse box. Furniture was transferred to London for use at the next IVSP centre. Bottom left photograph: Leonard Gray (standing on right)

CHAPTER 3

GODRIC BADER
Conscientious objector in World War II

Godric Bader is a member of Wellingborough Local Meeting. He joined the Friends Ambulance Unit during the Second World War and has been an active peace campaigner ever since. In 2009 Northamptonshire Quakers mounted an exhibition titled Quaker Roads to Peace. Godric contributed three placards dating back to the early years of the Campaign for Nuclear Disarmament. These fifty-year-old placards, together with a large archive of peace newsletters, newspaper cuttings and correspondence, were afterwards donated to the national Peace Museum in Bradford. Godric recorded an extended interview about his experiences of pacifism, published here alongside a selection of his photographs of the second CND Aldermaston March in 1959.

RECORDED PEACE STORY (October 2009)

Early influences towards pacifism

Can you tell me how and why you became a peace-maker? What are your earliest memories of the peace movement?

One very early memory that I recall... I was doing my piano practice in the front room of the house where we lived in Essex, I was able to look out of the window and see through the front gate the road outside, and in my imagination I would be able to rush to warn my mother, "It's come! there's gas rolling along the road!". Because I had obviously in my memory, even at that time, some background from the horrors of the First World War. My parents had experienced a concern at the time when gas and other instruments of war were becoming better known and understood. That's just a memory of the horrendous, horrific nature...of the need for peace to be developed.

Your parents sent you to a Quaker school, didn't they?

Yes, because there was nothing much locally around where we lived in Stanford-le-Hope, which was actually on a large area of its country outskirts called The Homesteads, something which Lloyd George had started... was it five, or three, acres and a cow? My parents had developed a strong attraction in that direction, having become vegetarians.

So were your parents convinced peace-makers, or pacifists?

Well not originally, I don't know that my mother was. She was more steady in the background, but they were both attracted somehow, when he came across from Switzerland, to hear talks and lectures on a wide range of subjects – I recall Zoroastrianism. He had this feeling that there was something more basic that he had to search for. I think he ran across, fairly early, Reginald Sorensen who was well-known for his work, particularly latterly in India. And there were a group that were speaking against the First World War around Hampstead, and some were thrown in the ponds at Hampstead Heath by the people there who were thinking: "This is impossible, we can't have these people who suggest that fighting the war is wrong!". And he got interested in that group somehow, because I think there was something fresh and alive which he hadn't quite experienced before... against something which he already felt was not a good thing, or he wouldn't have left the Swiss Army as he had done while doing his National Service. One Christmas he didn't go back. The sergeant who was in charge of the particular group he'd been attached to and he... said he would go to England and he wouldn't come back again. And he didn't, but of course he had already met my mother!

So really, peace was in your blood?

Yes, it was really. I do remember we had, fairly early on, a film projector. I remember seeing films of horrendous gas attacks, because that was, at that time, sort of equivalent to what we have now with nuclear weapons, and my parents showed pacifist films. That was the final gassing... it was seen by people to be a horrendous thing to do to anybody. How anybody could do this to anybody? That was the final stupidity.

Saffron Walden Quaker School

When you went to Saffron Walden School, did you have much contact with the peace movement there?

I can't think directly... yes, with Quakers. The peace movement did, I think, get talked about with the History master, a man called Stanley King-Beer, who had been a conscientious objector in the First World War. There was some background there that I suppose I probably picked up. We went to the local Quaker Meeting. The idea then was to take in to Meeting... if it was summer, you'd take a really noisy bee and put it in a match box and let it out at some moment or other, if you had the nerve to do it! And you did it in such a way that the masters or mistresses... one or two were settled around the group, keeping a good eye on you, and they wouldn't see who did it. I remember those sort of things! No, I can't remember any particular feeling of pacifism... but I was attracted towards it because of the background I had with my parents, and possibly I got some sort of... more of a deeper religious concern for it. In those days the Bible and other writings of Quakers were a background for deeper thinking... moving towards thinking that we have to do something about war. Because at that time we were worried that it was going to happen again.

So this was the 1930s, wasn't it?

It was the 1930s, yes.

Were any of your friends at school interested in what would happen if war broke out?

Yes, certainly. Three of them were: Proctor Le Mare, Ken Francis and I think possibly Stephen Walker. I can remember them discussing what they would do if there was a war. I think two of them said (including me) that they would probably not be willing to go into the Army. Stephen Walker, I think, was uncertain. I don't know where he ended up. But the other two did stick it out. Yes, certainly Proctor Le Mare was out in Yugoslavia at the end of the war with the Friends Ambulance Unit, which I subsequently joined, and Ken Francis worked on the land.

The outbreak of war

In 1939, where were you? Were you still at school?

I remember exactly where I was when war was declared. I was always interested in radio in one form or another, and I'd developed a rather sketchy kind of transmitter which would broadcast about two or three hundred yards, which was pretty good in those days. In fact I was under a plum tree, because it had a good aerial on it, and then I thought "Well, perhaps I ought to keep listening to the news." So I switched my equipment back to listen to the news and I actually heard the war declared. I can remember that very strongly. Certainly I was very concerned and quite worried as to how things would develop. I was still at school at that time. But I didn't know that my father had his house – the house where we lived was searched because of the fact that the neighbours had seen me transmitting to my cousin Brian Parkyn. They didn't know who it was, they thought I was talking to the enemy! When the police, or whoever they were, came to the house they found books in *German*. Well, this was obviously a spy, so Ernest was marched off to the local police station.

Not kept for long, I hope?

No, I think they soon realised he was no spy. But they couldn't believe there wasn't something behind it, somewhere or other!

Can you tell me something about your own experiences in the war years?

Well, clearly the blackout. And we had to move from where we were in the Thames estuary because we had – not actually air-raids on ourselves, because most of the German planes were flying in to the East End of London, or further if they could get there. But around us there were batteries of anti-aircraft guns going off on Laindon and Hornden Hills around us. During the night and during the day there were of course a lot of dog-fights and we had to go inside. I was out, naturally, watching what was going on in the sky. That was a dangerous thing to do! We did actually dig a shelter in the garden which we never used because it wasn't really suitable. But when we had air-raids we came down out of the bedrooms upstairs and collected under the piano, which was beneath the staircase where you were told you were more likely to survive. But we didn't actually get any bombs upon our property as such. We had a lot of bits and pieces from the anti-aircraft guns, one shell actually came through the roof at one stage. But we were lucky, there were houses further along the road that were actually blown up by Germans chucking out their bombs because they couldn't get as far as London. They just threw them out where they felt they would like to get rid of them.

Conscientious objection

So obviously keeping safe was number one concern, but what about concern over whether - or when - you were likely to be called up to fight?

I was prepared to face that, and I did get support from some of the background at the school. I remember that. I thought that I would be a conscientious objector because it was against the teaching of Christ, it was not Christian to kill your fellow men. There was a strong element of that, certainly. One should find better ways. That was the background. It was principally a fairly narrow-minded Christian approach – I say that now because I think the Christian approach can be very narrow-minded. When I came to the Tribunal in Cambridge later on, the statement I had to make did start off with the fact that I felt it was your Christian duty not to kill your fellow-men.

So you never really had any doubts about reaching that decision?

No I didn't. Really I felt I had to do it, whatever the cost. In spite of the fact that my coloured brother, that my parents had adopted before I came on the scene, was feeling that he would have to fight because he was in the local school and people there were doing what was normal, you joined the Army. I had to admire the way he cleaned his boots, because he was in the... pre-training corps, and you had to clean your boots at the front, you didn't clean them at the back because you never looked behind. You wouldn't look behind because the enemy was in front, you were going forwards all the time. To look behind was to retreat!

It must have been quite difficult to stand up as a conscientious objector in that period?

Yes it was, because of the elements of excitement of going to war and showing you were brave, and that you had the guts to fly a Hurricane or a Spitfire. It would be a fascinating thing to do. And shooting down somebody else, well if you had to do it you would do it. But then if you think about what you're doing, you would realise that this was probably not going to result in your conscience being satisfied as to what you were doing. Because it was against your belief that you shouldn't kill.

Where did you turn for support?

Well by then I had joined the university, Queen Mary College, London, that had been evacuated to King's, Cambridge. I felt I should join the Society of Friends because I felt there was... It's interesting this, I don't know if... probably my Saffron Walden background...I felt that this was a more acceptable way, because I wasn't too keen on the hymn-singing we had to do at school and also at the Methodist church in Stanford-le-Hope. It seemed to me rather pointless and narrow. I sensed there was something more fundamental that I should seek after, that would give me a more universal feeling: that it's the right way for people across the world not to get into these kinds of ways of looking at each other, and of feeling that there's an Enemy somewhere to kill and destroy. Also at that point it was partly the influence of my father coming from Switzerland, leaving another country, and feeling there was an Empire, and why wasn't the Empire creating a more peaceful

38

world and not going to war with the countries where they were involved?

Were most of the Quakers conscientious objectors?

I don't actually remember from the Meeting in Cambridge, but I certainly remember reading *Peace News* and other writings. I can't be specific about that. I sought support in talking to my friend Proctor Le Mare who felt like I did about the war, that we could be conscientious objectors, that we couldn't go to fight but we could do something to alleviate the suffering. And we had heard of the Friends Ambulance Unit and there was some interest in me, though I did start originally working on the land after my Tribunal in August.

Tribunal and farm work

What happened at the Tribunal?

You had to write out and state what you believed was right for you, and that was questioned by some formidable, important-looking people sitting on the normal bench of the magistrates' court, in a very important building – Cambridge Town Hall.

Almost like being on trial?

It was a bit like that, certainly. It was like that, and there was obviously a public gallery. A few people were there and the press could be there as well. I was helped a lot I think really by my father, who explained my background, and I think some of them felt, well, we couldn't expect this chap to do anything different. We could give him conditional exemption if he does something worthwhile.

Conditional upon..?

Doing either land, hospital – that kind of emergency services of some kind or another. Some people did in the war – what was it called? – "normal ambulance duties", but then you had to be in uniform and I felt I couldn't really be in uniform. There were other possibilities, not being in uniform, or being in the Ambulance Corps and helping people who had been damaged or killed, or refugees.

So you went to work on the land?

Yes, for a bit. Not for long. I do remember working – gosh, it was near Bristol – in a field which seemed... I remember it went on right to the horizon. I was with Michael Sorensen, who was the son of Reginald Sorensen who became Lord Sorensen and had been a great friend of my father. We were together by chance in a hostel and went hoeing – the farmer had given us the job of clearing a lot of weeds, and the weeds were taller than the plants, whatever they were underneath, we were salvaging a crop. I've forgotten the details but I remember working towards the horizon and it seemed endless to get this work done. We really worked extremely hard there, with blistered hands you had to ignore. And then latterly I was involved in going towards hedging and ditching, which was even tougher work, and at that point in time I asked for a change of occupation. I asked to join the Friends Ambulance Unit, because I thought this didn't seem to be helping an awful lot, on the land. In a way, you weren't doing anything... It was useful, yes, but you weren't doing anything where it was satisfying being more in contact, where you could be more of help, more directly with people who were suffering in one form or another.

Friends Ambulance Unit

Was it difficult to get accepted by the FAU?

Well, they had to be convinced that you were a genuine conscientious objector and you had good reasons for taking a stand. And you had to have a pretty tough medical examination. I remember the doctor made you put your hands on the back of a chair and jump up onto the seat of the chair twenty times! To see how you could do that; and then they would listen to your heart. If you could do that you were pretty fit. I think they probably gave COs a more severe one, in the sense of seeing how tough you were. Were you tough enough? Because these COs must be a weak-kneed, cowardly lot!

You had a kind of uniform in the FAU, didn't you?

40

No, we didn't, not an actual uniform. There was some kind of dress and badge which you had in common, but there wasn't actually an FAU uniform as such. When you went to hospital you had to have an orderly's clothes, of course. I was an orderly and I remember one particular matron shouting across to me, "Orderly! Where are you going and why?".

You've kept your FAU helmet all these years?

Yes. Well, the helmet we were issued with in the camp. We had a kind of toughening up and drill camp the other side of Birmingham, near the Lickey Hills – where we did our exercises which were largely training you up so as to be able to carry stretchers through very difficult situations, across rivers and up hills, in this case under branches and through forests, and going across fences in such a way that the patient on the stretcher didn't fall off. Things of that kind. It was a generally roughening and toughening up kind of exercise, and all of us who could drive were tested out.

Were they mostly Quakers in the FAU?

No they weren't. I don't think they were. There was a small percentage, but it was only about ten per cent or something like that.

So there were other conscientious objectors?

Yes there were, those Christians who just felt that somehow war was wrong and they had got conditional exemption somehow. But I don't remember having any grand discussions with them, of any kind.

Did you encounter any hostility or criticism because of your conscientious objection?

People turned away from you if they knew. I can't think of any – I'll think of some, some time – I can't think of any, because you tended to go with those people who were believing in you. I remember being billeted in LCC Hammersmith Hospital for further medical training. I tried to go to Kingsway Hall, where – what was that well-known preacher? – Donald Soper preached. That's what I did in the spare time we had, but we didn't really have much spare time. Of course we had to keep up our First Aid. We had to study and we had to pass pretty elementary examinations and tests. You had to have the hospital experience, you had to learn to inject, how to use a syringe, bandage limbs and that kind of thing. In the Oxford Wingfield Morris hospital my first exposure was actually doing the bed pan rounds. We had to wipe the bottoms of these poor characters who were in the spinal beds, just laid out flat and exposed to anything, and they couldn't do a thing for themselves. You had to do it all for them. That's when I did actually smoke a little bit, because the chap I did it with, who was a standard orderly character, said, "Come on, you do this, you do that, put this in your mouth, see, and you won't smell it so badly. Just keep smoking in the sluices!" It was also my job to empty and burn the theatres' rubbish.

Were the patients war patients?

Some of them were. I remember particularly an RAF character that had fallen out and been bashed up, and he was in dreadful pain all the time. It was very difficult to have anything to do for him. The worst one we had in that particular hospital was a farmer who'd been crushed by a horse trampling across him, that was a terrible damage. He didn't recover, but I remember shaving his face.

The Scott Bader Commonwealth and the peace movement

Let's move on beyond the war, to the 1950s. The Scott Bader Commonwealth was set up during that decade, wasn't it?

Yes, that was particularly important. My father read widely. He'd been influenced by fairly powerful reformist people that he'd read about, and in some cases met in London. Gandhi was obviously one. He had enough insight, in his ability to understand movements in the world generally. In the economic world there was a drive that he felt, and other people felt, led to war eventually because of the way the economic forces piled up and resulted in the need for the protection from a military background to protect the wealth of the capitalist elements which had created and fought for freedom to be able to build themselves up and have important power in the world. And the power had to be supported by military might. And this led – he felt – to the wrong kinds of attitudes that we should adopt to our fellow-men, to put it very simply.

So really, his business was itself part of the peace movement?

Yes, it was quite strongly. It's in the articles that were drawn up when the company was put into a charitable purpose in 1951. It was put in the charter that the company shouldn't get involved in war activities and products. Well, activities obviously because the company was making various things which could be used for war purposes, like the ingredients for camouflage paint.

Chemicals?

Yes, special polyester resins, particularly latterly for making radomes. That was a difficult one because they could also be used for civil purposes – in the ability of a plastic to let the radar beam come through and be analysed by the equipment inside, as against metal which couldn't have let the radar in, or would reflect it away. So we had to come to some kind of compromise. As long as the purpose of the product was for civilian application then we were... we would supply it as much as we could, in the sense that we would not be supplying it specifically for war purposes.

Were you working for the company in the 1950s?

Yes, I went to America in 1953. Was that the first time? Yes, I think it probably was, to get background and experience which included being blown up in a polymer explosion, so much so the whole plant was destroyed! As a result of that I was able to go across to the other side of America, to the West Coast, to California and San Francisco for sales and application experience. And I did go to Los Angeles and worked with the salesmen over there that had been selling the company's product which was coming from another factory. So I have some background in American salesmanship!

Campaign for Nuclear Disarmament and Bayard Rustin

Back in Britain, the Campaign for Nuclear Disarmament really got under way in the 1950s?

It got under way particularly because of the development of the Bomb. That was – I remember hearing it on the radio, listening to the explanation when it actually dropped on Hiroshima and then again on Nagasaki. That struck me as the ultimate stupidity, in the sense that this would develop in such a wide way, with the military mind that was still in existence, that the next war would be totally devastating.

How did you become part of an active, collective campaign around these issues?

Well I was incensed by people saying that we've got to have a bigger and better bomb in order to defend ourselves. I felt this was an ultimate stupidity because you can't defend yourself from something that's going to annihilate the world.

Do you remember the first anti-nuclear action that you took part in?

It was the second Aldermaston March. I missed the first. This was largely due – I was so involved in the company that there wasn't enough time to give to peace work, which I was clearly wanting to do. It was really the result of Bayard Rustin, an American negro Quaker who had been the second string to Martin Luther King and organised the 1963 March later on, on Washington, for freedom. Now I was interested in him, because he understood my situation with my black brother, and he was intrigued with that kind of a background, kind of a situation and how I was developing myself and my attitude to the fact that all men were equal and all men of whatever colour were valuable. I met him originally in the US through a Quaker contact, and then through actually going to Oxford. Yearly Meeting was held in Oxford that year, and I got very friendly with him. He was very educated, very musical – had a wonderful voice and was recorded widely in America for his

44

singing of negro spirituals. And he was interested in English background, and English life.

And in the little village of Wollaston, where we were living at that time, he actually went out and found some antiques. I didn't know that the village had any antiques at all, but he came back with, amongst other things, an illuminated Northants policeman's truncheon! While driving with him in Northamptonshire, we found a plague church that had been deconsecrated, the roof had gone, it was being used as a shelter for cows. There were some nice little figureheads at the end of the church windows, not any particular saints I don't think, but he was absolutely fascinated by these. What he actually did was to borrow a stonemason's saw and actually saw them off. Then he took them to America, literally holding them in his seat, to be quite sure that he was going to be looking after them well, and I think they've gone on to some museum in America. But it was rather exceptional and a pretty dangerous thing to do, if anybody saw you were cutting up a church, even though it had been deconsecrated! But it was right in the wilds, there wasn't a problem at all.

You had a lot of interests in common with him, apart from the peace movement?

I did, yes. He was a very cultured negro.

National and local CND campaigns

Coming back to the second Aldermaston March – what do you remember about that occasion?

Well I remember by that time my wife had got interested and felt certainly that the bomb was quite unacceptable. And she had met other women who felt similarly. They were a group going to Aldermaston with others, and I took them in the car there. And she was determined to march the whole way – and she did. I remember I slept on the floor – it was a pretty ordinary parquet floor – in one of the schools in Reading. That was the first stop, I think, from Aldermaston. Because this was on the Aldermaston to London, it wasn't like the original one which was from London to Aldermaston, to make the public aware of Aldermaston. That was why it went that way originally. Then it went back the other way, to London, to say "Look you lot, you've got to stop doing this, because this making of bombs is quite a stupid way of going on."

Did you go to the final rally, when they arrived in London?

Yes, my parents joined me there. There are photographs of them actually being there and my little daughter, at that time, was being held in the arms of my mother with Stanley Seamark, one of the big peace workers in Northampton.

Was this the period of the Committee of One Hundred?

That came later on. There was some concern that was a bit too radical, by one or two people – because they accepted prison many times. But of course, Bertrand Russell didn't think it was. Nor did Reverend Papworth. But some people thought that the things they did were a little bit too radical in the sense that they would get the public's back up. The public wouldn't understand the support for the Aldermaston March, so there had to be another way to prevent the bomb being used at all.

How did you feel about the Committee of One Hundred?

I admired their radical nature, their ability to do what they did, but I wasn't quite able to go to that degree of exposure I don't think. The people in London got the exposure, they were able to get the publicity they could do with in order to get the absurdity of having the bomb at all exposed.

You have given a placard from that period to the Peace Museum. Do you remember how you came to have that placard?

Yes, we borrowed some that we came across – I can't actually remember where – that were in the first March. We also improved upon them, then latterly they were helpful in demonstrating to the press, who understood the CND symbol, about the bomb. The particular middle-sized ones we had in Northamptonshire, intermediate missiles, they were short range, they weren't long-range missiles, but they were particularly placed, of course, to support America. America was really using us as a platform. They still do! It was absolutely stupid of the country to be so tied to the American bombastic way of life. If we'd got more linked with Europe we'd have had a much better chance of leading the world, I would have thought, in the right direction. Then it led on to Tony Blair and his stupid war in Iraq.

Though you weren't part of that London scene, there was a particular role for you here in Northamptonshire?

Yes. Northamptonshire was particularly able... according to Northampton not being further up in England, it was particularly seen as a good place to put missiles. There were several disused ex-World War II airfields here by then, that were still under the Ministry of Air probably, and they could be used straight away: Harrington, Polebrook, Luffenham, Alconbury. Harrington was the nearest to Northampton so there were continual demonstrations there. They were occasions that were agreed upon.

Who organised the demonstrations?

We started a local group representing Kettering, Northampton and Wellingborough. A CND group, yes. They were involved with those particular demonstrations. They were so exciting: you could actually see the missiles! They were ready to go off, you could actually see them standing upright. It was unbelievable. The local vicar – because we canvassed the area with leaflets, the villages around these areas – and one local vicar in Guilsborough said, "No, you're wrong, it's quite alright to use evil means against an evil country."

Russia?

Yes, it was Russia. Not only evil in that they had bombs and they were communists but they denied the purpose of God in the world.

Was the Northamptonshire campaign well-supported?

Yes, when we had a Pat Arrowsmith demo – where you would pitch a tent on government property. We had a supporting march from London, headed by Canon Collins of St Paul's.

Also I would guess we got about fifty people in a bus to Aldermaston usually, for the main March. Apart from correspondence in the press, there wasn't really any direct hostility. There wasn't any tremendous "ordinary local" support, the local papers gave fair reports and some good headlines, but there was a feeling that these CND and London people were probably a bit mad. They could see it was something that was important, but "We don't want to get involved..."

Did a wide range of people come to Aldermaston?

More respectable people, suits and ties also came along. There were quite a few women that were strongly involved. They were very vocal and very forward in their concern, because I think a woman's got an ability – a natural need – to be concerned for life at a deep level. Her instincts... I think some of them felt instinctively that to have a weapon of this enormous power was destroying something that they were responsible for: the creation of life. I think that's the way that Pat Arrowsmith felt, and others that were very well-known, like Vera Brittain.

Your wife Doreen was actually arrested wasn't she?

She was arrested for pitching a tent – which was quite ludicrous really, because the only time I got her into a tent (and I quite liked camping and that kind of thing, earlier in my life), she just got out and she made me get her into the local hotel! In that case it was a sub-aqua group that I was keen on and she had come along really for the interest, but she did not like swimming. No, she should never have been arrested for pitching a tent! The thing was, she stuck through it, and she went to jail. The tent was at the front of the base at Harrington, with the long supporting march from London. They were divided into those who knew they were going to be arrested, going to break the law deliberately – and she decided to join those – and the London march, which was concerned with just demonstrating and not getting arrested. It was quite large, quite a big group of people.

Were they aiming to set up a peace camp?

That was what they intended to do, but they didn't achieve it on the first occasion. Of course further on, Polebrook had a continuous camp. That was pretty much the one that stuck it through until very recently, but they had a convenient space which was neither government land, nor leased to the Americans.

It's good to hear that Northamptonshire had an active part in CND.

Yes, there were people from London that came, well-known activists who said, "We want to support you, you know. You've been supporting us."

Peace activism since the 1960s

You've never given up, have you? You've been active in lots of different ways since the early 1960s.

Well, writing letters... With money I'm able to help support the purpose and HQ office – you know, living simply and not living at the level I would have expected to live as a managing director and chairman of a small company, but nevertheless a company of some distinction in the work that was done in polymer chemistry. I've been able to give money for other purposes. I've been able to support CND and *Peace News* consistently, and of course Friends were doing quite a lot in that direction recently. And Pugwash in particular, I've been able to support.

What involvement have you had with Pugwash?

Becoming a member, and knowing something about it, and then going to some of their meetings... I was able to meet Professor Rotblat, in particular. He came to one of our Scott Bader Commonwealth lectures that we were having at Wollaston.

How do you feel about the peace movement today?

In a way it's sort of gone away, it's rather sad, because I think it's fractured. A lot of people felt that CND had pretty well done what it had to do, and have moved in other directions.

There's more support for small parts of what the peace movement has been doing, but I think the peace front is less developed, but more aware. I think it's a strange contradiction. It's gone into such activities as trying to blockade the recent arms trade fair – whatever you like to call it – which is, I think, particularly wicked because we're one of the, I think the third largest exporter and manufacturer of armaments. And this is something totally supported by the government purely for greedy financial reasons. I think it's a particularly wicked activity because clearly, without weapons the kind of trouble that's going on in Pakistan and other areas... honestly, these people couldn't do what they are doing without arms and explosives. They say they are not given arms. Arms are made by the West. They are supported and sold there. I mean, it's such a total nonsense!

I can see from your archive that you've supported the peace movement right across the board, many different organisations.

Yes, "Make War No More".

The Movement to Abolish War?

Yes, that's a recent one. And the Campaign Against the Arms Trade, War Resisters International, Peace Pledge Union, the Fellowship of Reconciliation, Peace Child, and recently the Ministry for Peace.

Are all the anti-war movements working in the same direction?

They are. I think it's rather sad that they can't make a broader front and have some of the guts that were shown originally, actually to sit down in Whitehall. There should be that number now that we could block off the offices that are concerned, the one in Whitehall that's concerned with war, the War Department or whatever it is. But you don't see that blockaded. I know that seems a bit extreme, and I don't know that I could do it, but I would still like to be involved in that kind of an activity. Even though we would risk – conceivably would risk – breaking the law and it would result in prison or other problems. But the reason why some people don't do it is because they know that it can lead to violence. Because it brings other elements in, like we've only had recently with the BNP.

The anti-Iraq War movement was immense.

That march... what was it, how many million?

Between one and two million?

Yes – and it was ignored. That disillusioned a lot of people, because they thought that if that number can march, it was going to have an impression. But it was ignored. So people thought, "Well we can't do anything about it, so why bother to keep up the pressure."

So you think its failure has been a setback for the peace movement?

Yes, I think it has. Peace has got to develop at a much deeper level. I think it is actually beginning to with certain younger elements. I feel it in younger people. You know, they don't think in any other way, than "Obviously, don't go to war." That's the way to find your way to create a peaceful world: "I don't want war in my life." You wear a white poppy because the red poppy is not doing enough, the red poppy is only remembering. We've got to do more than remember. We've got to create peace and not create remembrances alone.

Photographs: Aldermaston March, 1959

Godric Bader took this sequence of photographs during the second Aldermaston March in 1959. The March was organised by the Campaign for Nuclear Disarmament to oppose the spread of nuclear weapons. Hundreds of marchers made their way from Aldermaston, Berkshire, where nuclear warheads were produced, to Trafalgar Square, London. Among them was a strong Northamptonshire contingent, including workers from the Scott Bader Commonwealth and a group of women led by Doreen Bader, Godric's first wife. Doreen appears in a number of the photographs (below in the centre, wearing a white scarf). The home-made 'lollipop' placard "Nuclear Disarmament Northants" was carried for the whole distance, and is now at the Peace Museum, Bradford. An appliquéd fabric banner from Northamptonshire bore the now-familiar CND logo. Godric's parents, Ernest and Dora Bader, joined the March in London (final photograph, on each side of Doreen Bader).

53

54

55

CHAPTER 4

BRIONY AND HENRY MARTEN
Conflict in Northern Ireland

Briony and Henry Marten have both been members of Northampton Local Meeting for many years. They recorded this interview shortly before Henry's death in 2009. At the height of the Northern Ireland "Troubles" Briony and Henry spent fourteen years living in Belfast, where Henry was a university teacher and researcher and Briony was a school teacher. In their interview they reflected upon wider attitudes to peace and war, as well as upon their own experience as Quaker peace workers.

RECORDED PEACE STORY (August 2009)

Living in Northern Ireland

Briony: We went to Northern Ireland in 1965. We knew nothing about "the Troubles". We had three boys and Henry's boss went as Professor of Electrical Engineering, and Henry went with him as part of the team. And we stayed there for fourteen years until 1979. So that our youngest child, he was seven when we went there and twenty-one when we came back, which is a long time to be in Northern Ireland.

So you were really there during the worst of the Troubles?

Yes, of course it had been going on for years... I'll just tell anecdotes. I mean, we had a woman who was cleaning for us, a lovely, lovely woman who was

Briony Marten

with the Salvation Army. And I said something to her once about the divide of Ireland, and she said, "Ooh, let *them* have *us*..?" And her father had been wounded near where we lived in the 1920s. It just goes on and on and on... and she was such a liberal, lovely person, you know. Wasn't that extraordinary? English people would never have thought... I mean I was a mature student and my fellow students were about twenty-five or something, and some of them were Catholics and some were Protestants. The Catholic Church wouldn't let married women train as teachers, and they had never been mixed with Catholics (or the opposite) for their whole lives! So no wonder you had trouble.

The Protestant Workers Strike

Have you thought about some particular memories you would like to talk about?

Well, my main memory was of the Protestant workers' strike, what happened about the Protestant workers' strike. It was at the time when they tried to bring in power-sharing. It was...

Henry Marten

William Whitelaw. I don't know exactly which year it was, maybe 1974 or something like that. So, where I taught was East Belfast, and it was near the shipyards, Harland and Wolff, and by that stage almost an entirely Protestant area. It had been mixed. So one day the UDA – Ulster Defence Association – which was an illegal paramilitary, also political probably, they organised a strike to stop power-sharing. So my school... they forced the schools to shut down. They forced the children not to go. The children would have been in families influenced by this point of view – "In no way are we going to share power." I mean the slogan was a very odd slogan, but it was, "Ulster will fight and Ulster will be right", meaning Ulster will stay British and loyal and in no way share power with anybody who's a nationalist. So then came a day when the teachers at the school telephoned to each other – "what are we going to do?". I think it was most of the teachers, certainly the ones that I knew, we decided not to take our cars to school because they would have been hijacked, because a lot of hijacking went on. So we met near the school and parked our cars at this friend's house and we walked through these streets. Most of the children by this time were throwing stones at the soldiers from the barricades.

This was the Protestants?

There were no Catholics there by that time. There had been but there weren't by that time, they'd all moved out. We walked through the streets together, about six of us, and it was quite frightening really. As I said to you, we sang Ethel Smyth's song. You know: "March! March!" – we sang that. When we got there the only children who came to school were the Jehovah Witness children, because they were always different. They didn't sing the National Anthem, in all sorts of things they were always different.

They'd probably had a frightening walk as well?

They must have! So we had a very funny day with about three children in each class, and then I decided to drive home. I had a tiny little Fiat and I had to go through... By this time – I think that is what happens to you – I wasn't really frightened, I was just determined not to be bullied! It was a bullying situation. And when you came to barricades across the roads, the paramilitary people would sit on the front of your bonnet, and ask you where you were going, and even a friend of mine who was a District Nurse and who *had* to work that day, she got treated the same way. So then we went home of course, and life was not really very easy. It was – dear Mr Paisley was really very much behind it, he organised that the electricity workers should strike, so we had limited electricity. We didn't have power all the time.

Henry: It wasn't a complete turn-off.

Briony: No, and also they tried – I mean, to blow up the sewers, that was the next thing they were going to do.

So your witness for peace was to try and keep on with your work as a teacher?

Yes, yes... just not to give up.

Henry: During the Protestant workers' strike, somebody, some Protestant had understood that people were shooting from the tower of one of the churches in East Belfast, a predominantly Protestant area. And the local people thought that this wasn't good enough, that they'd got to do something about these Catholics that were established up this church tower, shooting at people. And so they got up a march, by advertising it and that sort of thing. And I happened to go along with this. I can't remember how I got involved, deeply involved. There was this march which consisted of a hundred people or something like that, possibly more. They were going to just march along the main road which went past this church tower, where the Catholics were ensconced and could shoot down. They were going to go and sort them out. And they were just getting ready to go, more or less, to start the march, when somebody with brilliant foresight said, "The only thing we can do to stop this..." Police were lined up across the road, waiting to try and stop these hundreds of people marching along the road. After which, of course, there would probably have been quite a lot of trouble. Somebody had the brilliant idea of asking Mr Paisley to see whether *he* could do anything to bring them to their senses. And so eventually, after they found Mr Paisley and persuaded him that he could help, he came and he addressed this crowd of Protestants. He said, "Don't you realise that this would be counterproductive? It wouldn't do your cause any good to go and attack the Catholics in the church tower." And he more or less saved that particular day!

Quakers and tolerance

Briony: The people I was with were all very liberal. I mean you did have to be careful what you said in Northern Ireland, I mean in social situations. You had to be careful because most people had lived there all their lives and they couldn't see much wrong!

So it must have been a very difficult situation to do active peace-making?

Yes, we kept quiet about it, we kept quiet about it. I can remember once we – the Catholics' houses were burnt down, before the Army came in. Once we went with furniture, mattresses and things to give to various people who had lost their furniture and I remember, very bravely a friend of my son's who was at school with him came with us into Ballymurphy, and his parents were *horrified*, you know, that he was going to do that, they were horrified. Most people we were not frank with, but the great thing was that we were members of the Society of Friends when we went there so we always had that support. We could always discuss things. I think one "witness for peace" was to listen to other people's opinions, but we weren't aggressively argumentative. We also gained strength from talking to people who did agree with us.

Henry: Protestants accepted Quakers, the Prods accepted them – that was because they thought they had grown out of the Protestant part of Ireland, stratum of Ireland or whatever. And during the Famine, Friends who had been quite successful as farmers were very... sort of generous.

They helped the victims of the Famine?

Yes, they helped the Catholics during the Famine. And that fact stuck with the Protestants, that they had done this – and also stuck with the Catholics. In those days they were careful not to discriminate against the Catholics, in the 1840s, 50s.

So would you say that both the Protestants and the Catholics had some respect for the Quakers in Northern Ireland?

Yes.

The Maze prison canteen and Ulster Quaker Service

Briony: The Quakers were asked to run the Maze canteen, where they started to intern people without trial.

Henry: Suspects... of being in the IRA. Yes, we knew of people being arrested and having to walk over glass, horrible things. So the government actually asked the Quakers to run this canteen. Of course the relations came from all over Northern Ireland, and they were just being bussed there and dumped. So the government built a place with a canteen and facilities, places where they could wait, and later there was a crèche there which was... I think it's now called the Monica Barrett Centre.

What part did you play?

Well we used to go and help...

So serving food and drinks, helping people – and talking to people?

Henry: Yes, and to some extent providing teachers.

Briony: And running the crèche. I wasn't there very much when the crèche was being developed. I remember people saying that the next thing there would be a Long Kesh university, there was so much being developed there really.

You were teaching in a Protestant area but helping Catholics in the Maze?

There were Protestant and Catholic detainees in the Maze. Only – we used to go there on Saturdays or something. Henry was involved in the Ulster Quaker Service it was called, wasn't it?

Henry: Yes.

Briony: It was really them who were asked to run this canteen.

So they were like QPSW (Quaker Peace and Social Witness), were they?

Yes, and they were supported by Quakers, and other people probably, from all over the world with money.

Henry: Including some from the Republic of Ireland, because there were quite a lot of Quakers in the Republic actually.

Briony: And America.

Henry: Some of the members of the Committee were well aware that one of the things that the clients, as it were, enjoyed was going out of their area to somewhere nice like the Mourne Mountains or the sea – all these things were quite close to Belfast. So we did what we could, and one of the things that we got was this minibus – we got the money from all over the place.

Briony: I'm sure the driver was a Catholic. I can't remember his name. The interesting thing about the minibus – a bit of Quaker history – was that two people came to help: one was English, Margaret McNeill, and Eileen Taylor, they'd both been at Woodbrooke and they'd both helped with displaced people after the War. You know a lot of Quakers did that. It was really their idea. And they had seen how wonderful, you know what a wonderful piece of outreach the Quaker minibus had been, and they were very keen to get one. And they were quite experienced really.

So once you got the minibus, who organised the trips?

Quaker Service, I should think.

It was your Committee, was it?

Yes, and we had a paid driver. They used to go into Ballymurphy, you used to take the children swimming, didn't you?

Henry: One incident I remember very well, I was driving the minibus at the time, coming down a well-known road in those days, the Falls Road – does that mean anything to you? I was driving this minibus with a group of Catholic children as it happened.

Briony: They were all Catholic because they all came from Ballymurphy.

Henry: Yes, I was taking them swimming you see, to do something they enjoyed. I was driving down the Falls Road, and there was a bit of housing beside Falls Road which was predominantly Protestant, and somehow or other the Protestant boys from this place got to hear that Quakers were taking children to the swimming pool. Doing work for the Catholics was not accepted very well by the Protestants. And I can remember going past this little section of the Falls Road with a collection of children in the back – I don't think there were any seniors. I think they were all Catholic children. And somehow or other news got around that there were Catholic children going past this little Protestant-dominated piece of the road, and as we were driving towards it we could see there were a group of boys on the pavement ahead of us. There wasn't really any option but to carry on. And they had accumulated a store of stones. They threw them at the minibus, with the Catholic children on board. They didn't actually do any serious damage, but that was more by accident than their intention.

Were the children very frightened in your minibus?

Somehow or other, I don't think they were, I don't know why.

Briony: The minibus had the Quaker star on it.

Henry: Yes, I think that's how they probably knew it, the Protestant boys. It was a white minibus.

Henry: I was very closely involved with the Ulster Quaker Service Committee. They now just call themselves Quaker Service. I think that's a bit presumptuous myself, but that's what they do. And they do the same sort of things, something to help the social problems that there are.

How did that fit alongside your work? I was wondering how you found time for it all? And what your colleagues thought about it all?

There were – a few of them were English, some of them were Northern Irish, and several of them were from the Republic, Irish.

Briony: We didn't mention peace work to some neighbours or colleagues.

Prejudice and rumours

Briony: Really, you can't talk about peace-making and your efforts without talking a little bit about the situation. I can add something about children. We used to have BBC programmes and sometimes a bit of news would come on while we were waiting for them, and it would say that some Catholic families had been killed. And these children – they were seven, nine, something like that – and they'd say "Good! More Taiges dead." They called them Taiges, slang for Catholic. "More Taiges dead!" It was absolutely shocking.

How did you deal with that?

I didn't dare say anything. I mean if you started spouting about the violence... Another thing that happened was that... Helen Campbell was a Quaker, and very much prominent in all this, and she used to say, it's a very well-known quote I expect, she used to say, "In war the first casualty is the truth." One day I was in the classroom and a plane flew over, in trouble – an RAF plane of some sort, right beside the windows of the school. This is rumours! At the end of lunchtime they all came back and said, "That plane was an IRA plane, come to bomb us!" - which was nonsense.

Henry: That's the sort of thing that happened.

Briony: Over and over again.

Other Quaker social work

Which Quaker Meeting did you go to?

Briony: South Belfast.

Did it have particular projects that it became involved in?

Briony: Yes. I don't know if you know about Will Warren. He came from East Anglia, alone. He was a Quaker hero really. He had a heart condition and he went to live in Derry. He lived alone in Derry, and he *knew* Martin McGuiness, he really... nobody would talk to that family or Martin McGuiness at that stage. We did have at one stage – we did offer refuge to refugees in our Meeting House.

Henry: This was a fairly well-defined incident. Early on in the troubles, the latest eruption. I think it – the little I know from first-hand – I think it's conceivable that the real shooting troubles grew out of the fact that at some point the group of

66

Protestants were living in an area which contained one street which was Catholic, and it was more or less isolated in this sea of Protestants. And some of the wise men among the Protestants decided that they didn't want them any more so that they went and burned the houses, they went and set fire to them. And the people living there, we don't really know exactly what happened to them, but we – the Meeting – actually housed them for a short period of time.

Briony: I think there were two separate incidents, but it doesn't matter.

They were refugees, basically, that you housed at the Meeting House?

Briony: Yes, and there were other places where houses were burned down. Different parts of town.

Henry: Yes, oh yes, but this was the first time that Friends got really deeply involved, because they took in the families, or as many of them as they could, Catholic families from this street, and protected them from any further terrible things. I don't know to what extent that fact got around. It was well-known to local Quakers of course.

Were you afraid of reprisals from the Protestants?

Well, yes – that was the thing.

Briony: The place where we lived was near Stormont, and pretty liberal. If you went further into town, that was the place where all the kerbstones were painted, red white and blue, flags everywhere.

Henry: They were loyal you see, red white and blue...as opposed to orange and green.

Briony: The only time I think I felt frightened was when our son was washing up in a Quaker work camp in a school and a strange voice rang up to check whether my son's identity was genuine.

What other work did Quakers do?

Briony: Let's think, well you certainly did the minibus and the Maze. The Maze was a full-time job for some. There had to be volunteers every day.

Henry: They used to provide transport for people living in the centre of Belfast, out to this Maze prison.

Quakers provided the transport?

Quite a lot, yes. They provided the transport there and back.

You say that resources came from all around the world. Was it a problem raising the money?

Briony: No, not at all, not at all. It was a well-known cause. Not at all.

Henry: I mean, Americans and Canadians, a lot of them are Irish.

Briony: I think the money flowed in actually. The money flowed in, and also we had a lot of... a lot of young people came, didn't they, volunteers.

Henry: And it's still going on!

I've heard you talk about Quaker Cottage.

Briony: Oh yes.

Was that founded when you were still in Ireland?

Henry: Yes, not very long.

What's it for?

It's a farmhouse, right on the outskirts, the edge of Belfast. Further down the Black Mountain from where Quaker Cottage is, is quite a large housing estate. A lot of the people living there have been transferred from troubled places. Most of them have got some problems of some sort or another.

Catholics and Protestants?

Predominantly, yes both.

Briony: That was the point.

So people living on the housing estate were invited to Quaker Cottage?

To spend... they used to go there several times a week, I think.

Henry: The way it worked was that Quaker Cottage was upon the social workers' list of possible places to take troublesome people, or people who had *troubles.*

What did they do when they went there?

Well a lot of them, the ones they took were women with children. I mean in comparison with some areas the people were fairly civilized. The children were felt to be at risk, of what I'm not quite sure, because the Cottage was in contact with the social work people, and they used to get women with, normally speaking, a few children – kindergarten age children.

Did you go to the Cottage, Briony?

Briony: I have been there once, just to visit, but I didn't work there. Well they have been taken up by Quaker Service, so they're supported by Friends all over the world.

Will Warren's Quaker peacemaking

When you were in Northern Ireland did you ever feel that there was anything Quakers could do to actually end the Troubles? Or was it always trying to help with the consequences?

Briony: You see, Will Warren was somebody who actually went into the politics, got to know Martin McGuiness, which was a *very* unusual and dangerous thing for anyone to do. I mean – it was very dangerous really. This is not really relevant, the most extraordinary thing is that Will was very supportive to our youngest son. Our son went and stayed with the McGuinesses and had breakfast in bed there, I remember. I mean they treated him as... Martin McGuiness wasn't there of course, it was his mother. We only realised later, Will Warren was a most extraordinary person. Books have been written about him, haven't they? He had a minibus as well, then he eventually had ours, and he used to bring mixed parties of children – take them everywhere! He didn't care what he did. He was just so...

Henry: I think most of the children came from Derry.

Briony: He came from East Anglia, just came. We did know him, he came to stay.

He was a member of your Meeting, was he?

No, I suppose he was a member of the Derry Meeting. We knew him and of course he was supported by lots of people in our Meeting. Just one of those people who gets up and goes, you know.

Different Quakers, different views

Briony: I think one of the things that was interesting... You know the powers that be in Northern Ireland asked the Army to come in eventually, to stop the Catholic houses being burnt. And we went to Meeting the next day, and nobody said anything about it. I can't remember anybody saying anything about it. It was a very controversial situation, wasn't it? I've always wondered why. I can't remember anyone saying anything about it. One Friend was more supportive of the IRA situation than other Quakers. She would say that there were two armies, the IRA and the British Army. That they were right, I suppose. So there were different opinions. What it really meant was that it absolutely took over the Meeting. It was *the* concern of the Meeting, wasn't it? And you wondered whatever people were thinking about in England, you know. It just took over.

Henry: Well in the original Meeting in Belfast, which started probably in the 1700s or thereabouts, its members were traditional Protestants.

Briony: They were Huguenots.

Henry: But then, largely at the instigation of two or three members of the congregation, they decided, these few members, that they wanted to bring peace, that they really did. The Meeting we went to had a large amount of English influence.

Briony: It was a breakaway.

Henry: From the locals.

So having an English influence, what was that? Was it from the University staff?

Briony: The University staff and some other people. We had some locals.

I think it's very interesting that different Quakers had different feelings about the Troubles.

Yes. I think you'd hear somebody saying something different. Of course there were the very, very evangelical country Meetings as well, they were different, used to get up and say about being saved by the blood of the Lamb and all this. The "country" Friends were more evangelical and more Protestant in Northern Ireland terms, which meant they probably did think of two different communities. The incomers like us – and there were others – had no axe to grind so it was easier for them to be tolerant. The incomers were less inclined to think of Protestants and Catholics as two communities than some locals, even amongst Quakers.

Were all the Quaker Meetings united in supporting the Peace Testimony?

I imagine so. I imagine so, but some went further than others I suppose. It was a whole "them and us" situation you know, when some are going to think "them" are worse than "us", who are wonderful.

Frightened underneath

So after you came back from Ireland, did you keep in touch with what was going on there?

One of the things was that we used to come here sometimes for holidays, and although you were fairly calm when you lived there... You did seem to have ordinary lives. The children went to school, and you had ordinary lives, and you didn't talk about it too much. It was kept from children quite a bit, what was going on. But when we used to come over here for holidays sometimes, you just realised how frightened underneath you were, all the time. I can remember being in Marks and Spencers once, here, when there was a sudden puff up of smoke... And the sort of stupid things like, if you see a stray car parked in a street, in fact a parked car which had a Northern Ireland number, you came and asked what it was, where we went to live in Greens Norton. And people were really, they were *remarkably* calm, remarkably calm. I can remember a hijacked bus with a bomb in front of a shop you know, and people just walked out. Another thing, our attitude, I can remember coming home from holiday, from the South somewhere, and they said, "Oh there's a hoax bomb in that street, you'll have to go a different way." And you just went, "Don't think about it, just go a different way!" And I can remember another time, a sniper – hearing a sniper. Well I was terrified, but all the other Friends were frightfully straight up, British sort of thing... I was terrified!

Looking back

I know that after your years in Northern Ireland you did other peace work?

We did supporting refugees in Northampton, which is really "them and us" as well, isn't it?

You'd had experience of that already, hadn't you?

Yes. I mean you just thought it was daft, the whole thing...

Where were the refugees from?

Somalia mostly, and that wasn't particularly Quaker, it was more the Justice and Peace Committee. But you know you did just think it

Left to right: Briony Marten, Theodore Sturge and Roger Sawtell at the Northampton peace vigil

was... I mean we couldn't see why Ireland shouldn't be united. You know, we couldn't see that at all.

Did your views on Ireland change while you were there?

I think English people were very ignorant about the situation, and thought they were all crazy. They thought it was all a religious thing, and it's more than that. They thought, "Why waste all that money on Ireland?"

Had you been to Ireland before you went to live there?

Yes. What did Dennis Barrett say about Ireland? He wrote a book.

Henry: Well, one of the best known sayings within it was: "The Irish have a problem for every solution."

Briony: Of course, he was in our Meeting and he did a tremendous lot, didn't he?

Henry: Yes, he had been born there.

Briony: The people that I really admired were the people who had been brought up there and who had thought very, very differently. They were behind reconciliation and just didn't think in terms of "them and us". And there *were* some of them!

CHAPTER 5

RAY HAINTON

Campaign for Nuclear Disarmament

Ray Hainton has always been committed to peace and internationalism. Since 1980 she has lived out this commitment through her work for the Campaign for Nuclear Disarmament. Her CND work has taken her to the USA and USSR, as well as to Greenham Common, Faslane and Aldermaston. She wrote a chronology of her peace work to help her prepare for this interview.

Ray Hainton (left) with family members.

RECORDED PEACE STORY (September 2009)

Joining the peace movement

I've always been concerned about peace and disarmament, even before I became a Quaker in 1969. For example I started a branch of the United Nations Association in Hounslow in 1956. But I didn't become involved with CND until 1980. I went to a weekend at Woodbrooke, the Quaker College in Birmingham, about disarmament, in the Easter of 1980 when cruise missiles were coming in. And it wasn't until then that I realised the full horror of nuclear weapons and the fact that the theory of mutually assured destruction was being replaced by talk about a limited nuclear war in Europe. I was so horrified by all this I went back to East Cornwall and started a peace group in Tavistock. It was then that I met Bruce Kent. I went up to London to find out material for running a peace group and met Bruce Kent, and then held a meeting in Tavistock and we decided to call it the Tavistock Peace Action Group. And the first thing we did was hold a public meeting to show the film 'The War Game' which was banned by the BBC. And we also ran a float in the Tavistock Carnival.

Did you have a large group of supporters?

I think there were probably about twenty of us, very enthusiastic. Some of them were Quakers and some of them weren't. We got the Quaker Peace Action Caravan to come to Tavistock and we decided fairly early on to affiliate to CND because they were the people who had all the information. And we got a coach to a demonstration in London in 1981 and were astonished that a quarter of a million people turned up. It was against nuclear weapons in general and cruise missiles in particular.

Visit to the United Nations

Fairly early on you started to travel abroad for peace campaigning?

We decided to support the World Disarmament Campaign which was collecting signatures to go to the Second Special Session of the United Nations Disarmament in New York in 1982. It was asking people to sign, begging the Powers to disarm in general. And Bruce Kent took a party of about fifty to the Second Special Session in New York, and I went on that. It was very impressive. We marched from Central Park past the United Nations building. Actually the march was just asking for a freeze on nuclear weapons but there were about a million people there from all over the world and the World Disarmament Campaign had collected signatures from all over the world. They got about four million signatures and I watched Fenner Brockway present these signatures to Perez de Cuellar, who was the Secretary General of the United Nations at that time.

Did you talk to peace campaigners from other parts of the world?

Well there were people from all over the world. I was particularly impressed by the Japanese. I remember they gave us garlands of paper cranes. And I was very impressed by the Native Americans as well.

What were they doing?

I just went to one of their meetings which was very strange to me. I can't remember the detail now, only that I was, I think, the only white person there in fact, and they were carrying out strange rituals.

Greenham Common

The same year, you visited Greenham Common?

We took a coach from Tavistock to the women's demonstration at Greenham Common just before Christmas in 1982. And we did take men as well, they weren't supposed to take part in the demonstration but they were there in a supporting role. I joined in with the thirty thousand women who held hands and embraced the base. We stretched all round this great fence which is nine miles long and we decorated the fence. I put up pictures of my grandchildren and people were putting up baby clothes, and I remember as we drew away... It was nearly Christmas time so it was dark by four o'clock, and we had lit night lights all round the base. I can still remember how impressive it looked.

Did many people from Tavistock go?

Well we filled a coach, yes. People of all ages, lots of young people.

What was it about Greenham Common which particularly roused people to protest?

Well that was where the cruise missiles were based. They hadn't actually arrived, but that was where they were first based. And these women had marched from Cardiff and were camping outside the base and said they were going to stay there until cruise missiles went away.

Why do you think women particularly got involved in this campaign?

Well they started by calling themselves "Women for Life on Earth". I think, as women who give birth to life, they felt particularly strongly against the horror of destroying it indiscriminately.

Had you been involved in the feminist movement?

No, I wasn't at all really an ardent feminist but I could – having children and grandchildren – I could see what they were driving at. In fact they had a slogan: "Take the Toys From the Boys".

Talking to the Russians

After Greenham Common you travelled again?

I made several visits to the Soviet Union as it was then, first of all in 1981. All these visits were organised by Quakers. 1981, I went on a trip to Moscow and Uzbekhistan and Leningrad. And it was organised by Sidney White, a Quaker from Birmingham who's dead now. Of course the Russians had invaded Afghanistan the previous year, so Russia was the "great enemy" all these nuclear weapons were aimed at, and Sidney White's idea was that we ought to talk to the Russians. So we did. We actually visited peace committees in Moscow and Tashkent and Leningrad. And I went on another such peace trip to the Caucasus in 1983. We went to Baku in Azerbaizhan and to Tblisi in Georgia and Yeravan in Armenia, and met peace groups. And the third trip to the USSR I went on was organised by Eleanor Barden, a member of Northampton Quakers. It was called "Meet the Russians" and we stayed in Moscow and met a lot of Russian families.

What was the aim?

Well, to meet the Russians and get to know them as people.

Did you speak Russian?

Well I started trying to learn Russian, in fact I persisted for a good many years but I'm afraid I haven't kept it up. I did learn a bit of Russian. My aim was to be able to talk to the Russians in their own language. I did learn a bit of Russian, but really you have to work at it every day and I was so involved in other peace activities, and being old I think it's harder to learn, so I never really mastered the language. I gave several talks after my Russian journeys on "Is There a Russian Threat?". I came to the conclusion there wasn't, and said so! There was a certain amount of hostility. I remember this talk was advertised in Wimbledon, and we had people throwing bricks through the window. I never saw them. Some of the members of the Wimbledon Peace Group chased after them, I don't think they caught them.

Faslane

During the 1990s you became very involved in the campaigns around Trident missiles and eventually the campaign around replacing them?

Well I organised a trip to Faslane, where the Trident submarines are based on the Clyde, from Exeter.

What did you do there?

Marching past the base, making speeches at the main gate. There have been a lot of blockades at Faslane but on that occasion there wasn't a blockade.

Campaigning in Exeter

Arrest at Aldermaston

In 2000 I invited Angie Zelter, who runs the Trident Ploughshares campaign, which aims at taking non-violent direct action against Trident. I invited her to come and speak in Exeter. And she was so impressive – she was inviting people to come and join the blockade at Aldermaston – that I did go with four others to join in this blockade.

What were they aiming to do?

78

Well, to stop people going to work at the base. Aldermaston is where the nuclear missiles are actually made – the warheads, not the missiles. The warheads are made at Aldermaston in Berkshire, the missiles are actually made in the United States, then they're put on submarines which are based at Faslane. Anyway, the aim was to stop people going to work at the Atomic Weapons Establishment at Aldermaston, and they start work at half past six in the morning. We slept at Douai Abbey which was two or three miles away and got there before half past six, joined ourselves together and lay down in the road in front of the main gate, to stop people coming to work.

How did you feel?

I had never done anything like that before, though I'd been to a lot of demonstrations outside bases. I can remember the policeman in charge saying he really didn't want to arrest us – "Please go away". And we were cleared off the road by the police, then we ran back and I think I felt a bit frightened. Anyway I did go back and I was arrested and dragged off the road, taken to a police van, then to a police station some distance from Aldermaston. I think the Reading police station was full up because there were an awful lot of people, so they had to use this other police station which was quite a way away. I can't remember the name of the place now. Anyway I was searched and they took away my money and all my belongings and put me in a police cell. And you have to take your shoes off before you go in a cell, in case you might strangle yourself with the laces! And I can remember the door clanging, and I realised what people mean by talking about being banged up. But I was given a piece of paper saying I was entitled to a blanket and a pencil and paper and food. They did offer us a choice of food. I asked for the blanket and the pencil and paper. The place was wall-to-wall concrete. I couldn't see you could possibly hang yourself, even if you wanted to. There wasn't anything to attach your bootlaces to.

I spent my time writing an account of this for the Exeter CND newsletter. I was left for some hours, but finally let out. The policewoman that let me out of the cell said, "Was I the one who wrote for the Exeter CND newsletter?" I was very surprised that she should know that. I was hauled before some senior police person, and she was up on some sort of platform and I was down below, obviously meant to feel very small, and at a distance. I said "I'm sorry, I can't hear you. I'll have to come a bit nearer." Anyway she told me I was being released on police bail, and that I would have to attend Newbury Magistrates Court. After which I was let out, and people at Aldermaston had organised a system of cars to come and fetch people who were let out. I was met and taken back to Aldermaston. My friends were very pleased to see me.

I was kept dangling, so to speak, for some months, and then I was told I had to attend Newbury Magistrates Court at 11 o'clock in the morning. I was living in Exminster by that time, but I couldn't possibly get to Newbury by 11 o'clock in the morning. I was wondering how on earth I was going to do it, but eventually after about three months I received a letter saying that the Public Prosecutor had decided it was not in the public interest to prosecute me. I think really the authorities were getting a bit tired of old women standing up in court saying why they were lying in the road at nuclear bases. But I must say this: being arrested gave me more publicity than anything else I've done in the peace movement. I was very surprised when I went down to the village shop to see a big placard outside – newspaper placard – saying "Exminster Gran arrested"! People had seen me driving round the village with CND stickers for years and had never discussed the matter, but after this they all wanted to talk about it.

How old were you when you were arrested?

Seventy-eight.

Was that the reason you decided to be arrested – because it would attract more publicity?

No, I think it was because I was very impressed with Angie Zelter. I felt she needed support. I was quite surprised at the amount of publicity it did attract.

Exeter Peace shop and the Iraq War

In the 1990s we had the first Gulf War, then in 2003 the Iraq War.

Yes, I haven't said that I moved to Exminster in 1986, from East Cornwall and the Tavistock area. And I obviously joined Exeter CND, which was much larger than the Tavistock group, and quite soon became the secretary there.

Can you explain how the CND campaign developed in connection with the Wars? And talk about the Exeter peace shop?

Well, Exeter CND had opened a peace shop quite early in the 1980s, before I moved there.

What is a peace shop?

Well, our basic aim was to give people information about the peace movement. But I mean the shop is still running. It sells peaceful goods, a lot of peaceful toys in particular, and campaigning materials, T-shirts and banners and mugs and badges and posters and it also carries a lot of information about peace issues and the environmental issues as well. And petitions, and on the run-up to the Iraq War in 2003 the peace shop became the centre of the peace movement in Exeter. We worked very closely with the Stop the War coalition. And there was so much opposition to the Iraq War, our little shop became full of TV crews and the phone constantly going with journalists wanting information. And we actually ran twenty coaches to the big demonstration in London on the eve of the Iraq War. We sold the coach tickets at the peace shop.

Twenty coaches from Exeter?

Twenty coaches from Exeter, yes. It was very hard work.

What part did Exeter Quakers play in the peace movement at that time?

Well, a lot of them did go on the coaches.

Was there any other peace work going on in that period?

I didn't actually go to that London demonstration because some people who couldn't take coaches to London asked me if we could have a demonstration in Exeter. So I decided there were so many people going to London that I would organise a demonstration in Exeter High Street, which I did.

This wasn't an anti-nuclear demonstration, so how does it link up to CND?

No, well CND has always worked closely with the Stop the War Coalition and also the Muslim Association of Britain, and it isn't simply an anti-nuclear movement. It is an anti-war movement and there is always a danger that nuclear weapons will be used in these wars of course. In fact Geoff Hoon, who was defence secretary at the time, actually spoke about the possibility of using nuclear weapons against Saddam Hussein.

Changing public opinion

Your long experience of peace work – has it been worthwhile? Has it been effective?

Well we did get the cruise missiles out of Greenham eventually. In fact Greenham Common is back to common land, and we are working for an international convention to abolish *all* nuclear weapons. And I feel more hopeful now about the possibility of that than I have done for the last twenty years. We held a lot of street demonstrations in Exeter, giving out leaflets and collecting signatures, and I spoke in several schools and colleges. Younger people than me have been speaking in schools. I think it has had an effect on public opinion. I have seen a change in public opinion. People used to say to me, "Nuclear weapons have kept the peace for forty years." You don't hear that any more, and I saw in today's paper... a poll conducted by the *Independent* newspaper yesterday reported that 58 per cent of the people polled think we should get rid of Trident. So I think we are gradually changing public opinion. And I think in the long run the government will have to listen to public opinion.

CHAPTER 6
ELEANOR BARDEN
Meet the Russians

Eleanor Barden is a member of Northampton Quaker Meeting. She worked with other British Quakers and Russian colleagues to open up communication between ordinary people in Britain and in Russia during the final years of the Cold War. This written account was prepared in the Northamptonshire exhibition 'Quaker Roads to Peace' (October 2009), and presented alongside Eleanor's extensive collection of photographs from that period.

Eleanor Barden

PEACE STORY

In 1986 Gorbachev came to power in the Soviet Union, and introduced some significant changes in the situation there. Grace Crookall-Greening was then working in the Peace Department at Friends House, as Assistant Peace Secretary to Ron Huzzard. She had visited Russia at least seven times on behalf of Quaker Peace and Service, and was anxious to take advantage of the changed situation there resulting from the appointment of Gorbachev. I served on the Peace Committee at Friends House at that time, and Grace discussed with me her idea that we should encourage groups of Friends to consider visiting the Soviet Union. I had for some time been receiving groups of students from abroad, who visited this country to attend courses on the English language that Ron and I organised, and I had also been learning Russian, so I agreed to organise a visit to Russia for those interested.

My late father had been a very successful Trade Union leader, so I contacted one of his colleagues, who put me in touch with a Russian Trade Union leader, Teiyar Tariverdiev, who agreed to make all the necessary arrangements for me in Russia. William Barton, recently retired as General Secretary of Friends World Committee for Consultation, who also spoke Russian, accompanied Grace and me on our visit to Russia to meet Teiyar and discuss our requirements, and Teiyar took care to meet our wishes exactly, and did everything very well. We sent groups of Friends, who were always accompanied by a Russian-speaking English group leader (I remember group leaders William Barton and John Holtom – but there were others) – all accommodated and well cared for by Teiyar and his colleagues. I also had contact with Tatiana Pavlova, a Friend and friend of mine, who lived in Moscow and invited Russian friends to attend meetings for worship in her home. Tatiana was happy to make contact with the visitors we sent to Russia. So our teachers met Russian teachers, businessmen

Meeting the Russians: Eleanor Barden in the
centre, right-hand side of the table.

met Russian businessmen, musicians met Russian musicians, and so on, and all seemed well satisfied with the arrangements made for them.

After a while, I was asked by Teiyar if we could accommodate and make an interesting programme for groups of Russians who would like to visit our country, stay with families, and go sightseeing, which I agreed to do – and this also proved very successful. And I liked to think that it helped to improve relations between our two countries! We continued sending groups to Russia for some years, but as relations with Russia gradually improved, demand for this specialist service for Quakers reduced, and we finally gave up the work.

CHAPTER 7

KELLEY REID

Conscientious objector, Vietnam War

Kelley Reid is a member of Wellingborough Quaker Meeting. He has lived in Britain since 1997 when he moved to London from Seattle, Washington, USA to take a job at the American School in London. He now lives in a small Northamptonshire village with his wife Julie.

PEACE STORY

As my eighteenth birthday approached in February 1968, I received a notice from the draft board requesting my registration for the draft. I was living in Chicago, Illinois, at the time and my country was at war.

Knowing I would receive a student deferment to attend university the following autumn, and being fairly conservative in my political views (in keeping with those of my father), I registered without a great deal of soul-searching.

However, as with many of us coming of age during the Vietnam era, I soon began deepening my awareness of the conflict. This, in turn, led me to other questions about myself and my place in the world. I began to think more deeply about peace, social

Kelley Reid in the 1970s

justice and personal responsibility. And I began to rethink my registration for the draft. In this search I discovered a number of supportive resources, including the American Friends Service Committee and the Bahai Faith, actually becoming a Bahai in 1969.

As a Bahai, I requested, and received, a change in my status, becoming a conscientious objector, but remaining eligible for the draft. Had I been drafted, I would have served as a medic or in some other capacity where I didn't bear arms.

However in 1970 I gave up my student deferment and became part of the first lottery of the Vietnam conflict. I remember well the night they drew birthdays out of a barrel, determining who would be called when, from first to three hundred and sixty fifth. My number was something like two hundred and ten. That year the war machine only needed young men up to the number two hundred and six. And, as the war was beginning to wind down, I was never drafted.

CHAPTER 8

THEODORE STURGE
Peace vigils and peace witness

Theodore Sturge is a member of Northampton Quaker Meeting. He is a birthright Quaker and has been actively involved all his life. His family have been associated with the Religious Society of Friends for many generations.

PEACE STORY

My father was a conscientious objector in World War II. He was totally unwilling to kill. He did not talk about it very much, but as a young teenager I

Theodore Sturge

remember being in a town centre somewhere away from home where there was a silent Quaker peace vigil taking place. He told me to go off on my own, and I can still see him quietly slipping into the line of Quakers, and those already there parting so that he was absorbed into them, no questions, just a quiet acceptance that here was somebody of like mind who would witness with them.

Most of my adult life I have been involved with peace vigils and peace witness. In Leicester I was involved with the Campaign for Nuclear Disarmament and regularly organised the stall in the Market Square on Saturdays. I did this in conjunction with Leicester Ecumenical Action for Peace. With this group I also helped to organise interdenominational events and hustings when there was general election. The Quaker Peace Group held monthly vigils in the Town Hall

Square. We usually had a letter for the public to sign and I remember one at the time of the Falklands War when the Belgrano and HMS Sheffield had just been sunk. We were saying, "Both sides have now proved they are serious, the terrible killing on both sides has to stop. Pull back now while you still can." I took the letter back to the museum where I worked prior to posting it and every time I stuck it up to take it to the post another member of staff made me open it so they could sign too, saying "That is just how I feel too."

Later, I worked at the museum in Coventry. We had a peace garden outside the museum which had recently been opened by the Queen Mother during the events to mark fifty years since the Blitz. During the First Gulf War I gathered a group of colleagues around me and every lunch time we held a silent peace vigil around a candle in a jar. One day Canon Paul Oestreicher from the Cathedral came past; on his return he presented us with a roll of Polos. He just said "Mints for Peace" and passed quietly on.

These days I prepare the posters for the Monthly Vigil on the first Saturday of each month in Abington Street, Northampton. My speciality is getting everything together so we have all the posters to put up so others can come and join us. We aim to make people pause, perhaps only fractionally, and think. The vigils are under the umbrella of the Northampton Christian Network for Justice and Peace. There is a strong emphasis on justice. Justice has to come first: you cannot have peace without it. Most people appear to ignore us, but who knows? We have a sign inviting the public to join us. Occasionally they do, or they stop and speak to us. We had two lads from the Forces who were going back to Afghanistan. One said, "What are you praying for, it's a stupid waste of time." We started to talk to them, and the other, quieter one said "Maybe there is something in it", and told the story of an officer in the First World War who prayed with his men at the start of every day. At the end of the War every man came home.

When numbers were low we were asked if we wanted

to go on. I said that if one other wanted to stand with me, I would continue. Somebody said "I will", and on it goes. An elderly Quaker comes in every time from Nether Heyford because she *has* to.

CHAPTER 9

FRANCES KEENAN
Teacher in Lebanon

Frances Keenan is a member of Kettering Quaker meeting. A Scot born and bred, she has lived, worked and studied most of her adult life in England, notwithstanding six years in Australia in the 1970s. Her spiritual journey, likewise, has traversed sectarianism and crossed borders to find Ecumenism wearing a Quaker hat!

Frances Keenan helping a Lebanese student

PEACE STORY

Reflection: Peace means the same in any language

I feel blessed and privileged to have had the opportunity to work as a volunteer teacher and Friend in Residence (in my early 60s) at Brummana High School (BHS) in the Lebanon for the 2008-09 academic year. I can honestly say it has been both a spiritually enlightening and culturally edifying experience for me, for which I am profoundly grateful.

That said, my first and last impression and feeling was of a profound and lasting sadness that permeates this war-torn country even though the friendliness and *joie de vivre* of the Lebanese in general, and multi-national students at BHS in particular, was often quite overwhelming. However, digging deeper at the personal level revealed the awful scars of years of conflict: the fears, stress, suffering, loss and anger amidst an incredible determination that Lebanon was not going to be occupied again and that their culture, heritage, religions, cuisine and way of life were theirs to celebrate and protect by whatever means. The loyalty of students to their school and friends within it was clearly genuine and very important to their lives. These students included Lebanese day pupils along with the boarders from across the Middle East, with some from Europe, Asia and America: both Christians and Muslims of many sects. I think it would be incorrect to say that BHS today is a Quaker School, but it certainly is one based on Quaker values, ethics and practice despite all the upheavals and traumas of years of wars that has damaged people's lives, well-being, trust and hope, as well as the infrastructure, economy, security, and institutions of Lebanon. The school motto – "I serve" – is respected, understood, valued and practised. Sunday Meeting for Worship is held within the school campus and kept alive by the relatives of the original founder (Theophilus Waldmeier [1832-1915] a convinced Quaker) and by Quaker visitors to Lebanon. Whilst students are noticeable by their absence at Meeting, it is wonderful to witness the population of multi-race, multi-faith students – rich and poor alike – all studying, playing, and socialising together during the week. That alone seems a valuable lesson for life: living peaceably and fruitfully with others and with difference. It was good to see several minutes of silent reflection practised before commencement at the weekly students' assemblies.

Enlightenment came from many unexpected discussions and quarters during my time in Lebanon. One was during a class discussion of 14-15 year olds when I was asked "Why had I come to Lebanon?" My response: "A golden opportunity at my age and also to be at the heart of where all the three great monotheistic religions started." The question that followed was not expected. "What – Christianity too, Miss?!" a Muslim student asked in amazement. I paused a minute before replying: "Well – yes, where do you think Jesus came from?" I continued "He came from Palestine and was a

Jew" (I paused) "but I realise why you might think that Christianity came from the West given the history of the Crusades in this part of the world." I knew that Muslims acknowledged Jesus as a prophet and holy man.

Moments of edification related to a poster I sent for, posted from Friend's House in London to BHS. The poster has a strong blue background emblazoned on top in white large letters with three words. First in Arabic "SALAAM"; in the middle in Hebrew: "SHALOM"; and underneath in English: "PEACE". Diagonally in small block capitals in pale blue are written in many other languages their words for peace. At the very bottom was a strip that said "Quaker Peace and Social Witness".

During the second term I took this poster to my Advisory class of Lebanese pupils (16-17 year olds) and asked them if they would like to put this on their empty wallboard, explaining that to achieve a lasting peace there was only one way and that was communication with all parties and this poster reflected that message. Then to my astonishment one of the female students shouted out – "What's that middle language?" (pause) "It's Hebrew we can't have that!" And then

Fierce Feathers: a play with a Quaker theme produced by Frances Keenan at Brummana High School.

there was a general and very noisy hubbub. So, raising my voice, I said, "If you want peace in this country then you are going to have to dialogue with the enemy. If you can't even look at the Hebrew word for peace 'Shalom', what hope have you got for the future? One of you, or maybe two in this class, could be a future Lebanese Government official. Think about this message, think about what war has done to your country and lives, there is only one way forward and that is talking in whatever language that it takes to achieve a future for you and following generations. And remember the words 'Salaam' and 'Shalom' come from the same root – they are both Semitic languages." I started to roll up the poster but the girl who had said "no" said, "We'll put it up as long as we can cross out the Hebrew word." I was pleased with the result, though shaken at what I had stirred and witnessed. The poster was up.

Then I was deported! The School Bursar worked with Securite Generale HQ and the Clerk of Meeting worked with the Lebanese Government's Minister of Interior to get me back. No-one apparently knew why I was deported, but my Embassy link was sure it was my family name, Keenan, and the apparent link to Brian Keenan of hostage history who had visited Lebanon for first time just before I arrived. The week before my deportation, a film of his life and times as a Lebanese hostage had been shown in West Beirut (Muslim area) which had upset a lot of officials. The combination of that, and also using short-term visitor visa to work as a volunteer at BHS (even though that visa system had worked for others), left me vulnerable.

Back at school with full clearance and bona fide visa – five weeks later – I took my other copy of the Quaker peace poster to Sunday Meeting. Afterwards, when the Clerk, a couple of local Quakers and an American Quaker lady visitor remained, I invited their thoughts about the poster. The reaction from the Clerk was so angry that I was literally dumbstruck with what he said. "How did I get this poster into the country – did I want to be deported again? Had I any idea what I was doing? This sort of thing might be alright in

Ramallah but not in Lebanon." And so on. The American lady said that she would give it to her son to use. The clerk said: "Under no circumstances – it identifies Quakers (QPSW) and we can't have Quakers allied to such a poster in this country." I realised then that he didn't know about the poster in my Advisory Class!

The next day I went to my class to take that peace poster off their wall board – much to their surprise. They said they were okay with it up as long as I did not mind the crossing out that they had done. I told them that was not the problem. I was in trouble about the poster from elsewhere which I could not discuss and I could not get them in trouble, or put myself in any more, so it had to come down – though I asked them to remember the message: *Peace means the same in any language; dialogue is a key weapon.*

Postscript

Subsequently I have learned that the Brummana Clerk had in past had a direct hit by an Israeli bomber on his home in Beirut. I had not meant to cause friction or upset – certainly not with the Lebanese Quakers or more importantly with the Clerk who had played a large part in getting clearance for me to return to Lebanon. I have, though, learned a lot from that fallout. The long term damage to peaceful negotiations between Lebanese, Palestinians and Israelis seems almost incalculable.

In my final weeks in Lebanon I twice visited Shatila "Refugee" Camp in Beirut. The stench of an open, festering wound will not leave me and I do wonder if this is an area where QPSW could, or maybe should have an active 'volunteer' presence?

CHAPTER 10

ANNE STREET

Peace work through aid agencies

Anne Street has been a member of Northampton Quaker Meeting since 1994. She is the Senior Humanitarian Policy Advisor at CAFOD (Catholic Fund for Overseas Development).

Anne Street

PEACE STORY

I am fortunate to be in a field of work which finds resonance in my Quaker roots. Before me both my parents did post-war relief work in Germany and one of my maternal uncles was the first pacifist in England to be officially recognised as a conscientious objector in World War Two. My paternal grandfather, also a Quaker, owned a small printing company where he printed pacifist tracts during the First World War. This lost him many customers and eventually his business folded.

All of them served as strong role models for me when I was growing up and I suppose that it is not surprising that I followed in these traditions and took up a career in international development. Initially I started working on human rights, which soon evolved to address peace and conflict issues working in Protection with refugees displaced by the liberation movement struggles in El Salvador and Guatemala in the 1980s. Subsequently I have worked for international NGOs as a humanitarian policy advisor seeking to influence the international policy agenda in relation to conflict and emergencies.

Part of that work involves listening to local people's concerns and trying to bring their voices to bear on the decisions made by national and international policy-makers. One example of this was some work I did on the United Nations Peace Building Commission. The PBC started work in 2006 as a result of the UN Reform process, and was set up in recognition that the UN system lacked an appropriate body to support and sustain countries coming out of conflict, despite the fact that over 50 per cent of countries emerging from civil wars during the 1990s fell back into conflict within two years of signing a peace treaty.

Through meeting with local people in the two focus countries of the PBC, Burundi and Sierra Leone, and hearing their stories, it became obvious that this kind of grass-roots reality was far from the knowledge and experience of UN diplomats and policy makers in UN headquarters in New York, who focused on stabilisation frameworks and peace building plans and analysis which were internationally driven without taking into account the views of ordinary people. Through detailed research and documentation of community experiences we were able to present some compelling evidence to the PBC's first year evaluation hearings of the need to re-focus the work of the Commission to take greater account of community level processes. The report we submitted contained recommendations which were then taken up by influential Member States and influenced improvements in the subsequent functioning of the Commission.

More recently, in late 2009, on a visit to Eastern Congo I met with a group of women at the Women's Sharing Centre in the Musavango 2 camp for internally displaced people. They spoke with pride about all that they had done in the last five years, despite living in frankly dreadful conditions – tarpaulin or plastic tents, barely eight foot by ten foot for an entire family. They had learnt basic literacy and numeracy, basket-making and soap production so that they would have a way of earning some money when they eventually return home to their mountain villages. They had shared psychosocial support as most of them had been brutally raped and left physically and emotionally scarred by their experiences. It was humbling to see their obvious pleasure in their shared camaraderie and their individual achievements. But best of all was the knowledge that whatever challenges they would face once back in their villages, the organisation I worked for had played a small part in making their future more secure by providing them with the skills to generate an income in what would surely be tough subsistence-level conditions.

I am mindful that there have been generations of Quakers who have stood up for their beliefs against prevailing orthodoxy, working for peace and social justice in the sure conviction that there is something of God in each one of us, and that through dialogue we can find a resolution to the differences that divide us. Although I have never been called to put my beliefs to the test in a way previous generations have done, I am fortunate to have them as my inspiration.